Loyalty Marketing

Managing Brand Loyalty and Customer Retention

Loyalty Marketing

Managing Brand Loyalty and Customer Retention

Updated in February 2011

Written by:

Nazimudeen Saleem

ISBN: 9 781446 617953

Published by Lulu.com

Dedicated to all loyal customers

Preface

Customer brand loyalty is a much talked about topic in marketing. In fact, one objective of any branding strategy remains to be building customer loyalty. Increasingly though firms employ loyalty card programs to retain the customer although genuine brand loyalty of a customer cannot be expected to be built through such strategies.

In this book the author takes a different view about customer loyalty altogether and considers it as a 'product' for exchange. It requires us to commoditize the concept of brand loyalty and sell it to customers. In this regard, in order to retain the customer through bonding, it requires the firm to offer something extraordinary in exchange for their long-term relationship. Such exchanges are not mere transactions and considered different to the traditional exchanges of goods and services for money. The title of the book therefore reflects the deep meaning of the concept of brand loyalty as a product.

Here the author sees the commodity called customer brand loyalty as something of an affinity and bonding that comes from the bottom of the heart of customers. Loyalty therefore does not come suddenly but may takes years to build up through meaningful relationships. Loyalty as a product therefore is said to have a life-cycle with stages of growth, maturity and decline.

Having defined and described brand loyalty, author goes to examine the issues of managing loyalty in order to recruit and retain customers. It requires the firms to build and manage customer brand loyalty by identifying and offering loyalty attributes. In this regard, Loyalty Marketing may seem like an investigation into the understanding of marketing orientation or customer orientation. Providing a new market segmentation model based on the attributes of the traditional marketing mix variables substantiates this argument. Moreover, this helps us to measure brand loyalty based on the attributes of customer loyalty and construct the brand loyalty life-cycle.

In a nutshell, Loyalty Marketing is about brand loyalty management and, therefore, it is obviously about strategic customer orientation. Although the book takes the reader deeper into measuring the intensity of loyalty and examining the analytical tools, the focus is on developing a customer brand loyalty management strategy. Author believes this will remain an essential book for all marketing professionals as well as for students. Brand managers, in particular, would find it very useful when it comes to formulating a customer loyalty management strategy.

London

March 2011

Table of Contents

Table of Contents

Table of Contents

Table of Contents

1 Introduction

Marketing Customer Loyalty: Who Would Want It?

It is fair to say that over the past century, marketing as a concept and its activities have made the consumers more sophisticated. Entrepreneurial freedom, market economy, and liberalization of credit have all contributed to the success of western economies since the postwar boom. With this there evolved a high degree of sophistication in consumption coupled with marketing innovations. In the meantime, technological advancement in production, logistics, and promotion have also encouraged new firms to enter the market easily. Although the market for a specific line of products of a firm could sustain to some extent due to increasing growth in consumption in general, only few firms would survive amid the emerging complex and competitive business and marketing environment.

Today, competing firms differentiating the product-service provisions to satisfy the sophisticated consumer expectation remains an accepted marketing activity here. In an increasingly competitive world of wild dogs preying for each other, winning a customer is, in deed, a difficult task. Then, what about retaining the loyalty of that customer, at least for sometime, if not permanently? For sure, customer turnover is costly but it is also becoming even difficult to win over new customers. It means the firms have no choice but to own the customer's loyalty at least for a reasonable period of time. Perhaps, you may want to call it 'leasing' or 'renting' customer loyalty. It means, recruitment and retention of customers remain crucial and, therefore, building and managing customer loyalty and formulating a branding strategy is an essential part of the marketing process.

Commoditizing Customer Brand Loyalty

The whole idea of managing customer brand loyalty is said to emerge from a new marketing philosophy of redefining the customer (or buyer) and the producer (or seller). This would obviously create a new marketing challenge and it is based on the assumption that the existing marketing concepts and theories are becoming obsolete and need of innovation in thinking. How about reversing the traditional concept of producer-customer or seller-buyer? It meant the customer becomes the producer or seller and the producer becomes the customer or buyer. Perhaps, you may want to call it a new marketing concept. Imagine that the customers have something for sale. Yes, a 'product' for sale, if you may wish to call it. And, who is the potential buyer? Of course, it is the producer firms that often try to compete with each other traditionally to sell their products and services to the customers. Whether you want to call this new concept a marketing revolution or not, it could indeed become a challenge for the marketers.

Then, does it make any sense to define customer brand loyalty as a 'product' for sale? Answer may be found in the following paragraph. Loyalty is an emotional baggage that customers build and carry. It is often based on the customers' perception of trust and confidence on a product (brand name) and or firm. Through loyalty, customer builds an affinity and sometimes becomes attached to a product or even a company's brand name. Loyalty derives from certain attributes of the product and or the firm that produces it (including the service elements associated with it) and it is often communicated through a powerful brand image. These loyalty attributes that are based on customer desires and expectations, determine whether the customer manifest any loyalty behavior.

Since these loyalty-attributes such as benefits and values sought are derived from customer expectations, it makes sense to package them and call it a 'product' for sale. This is what the author calls the commoditization of customer loyalty. Could this be a new marketing philosophy and marketing challenge? By commoditizing brand loyalty, a customer can claim that he or she has something to offer. If a firm desires to enjoy his or her loyalty, it has to offer those loyalty attributes in return. Of course, a firm cannot own customers' loyalty towards its brands or company itself forever. It is because firms do not always seem to show any reciprocal loyalty towards customers. Firms often talk about creating and managing long-term relationship with customers. But unfortunately, most firms see this in isolation, an independent strategy in itself that is distanced from customer loyalty issues.

Managing Customer Relationship and Brand Loyalty

Customer relationship management or CRM is a widely debated topic today. While businesses are beginning to recognize the importance of CRM and similar strategies, some seem to have engaged in debating the merits and values of adopting a CRM strategy. For some, CRM is a misunderstood buzzword accompanied by other closely linked sound-bites such as customer life-cycle or customer relationship life-cycle. In the meantime, there are some who have not explored the idea yet or even not heard of it. Some in the marketing world also have turned CRM into a software-driven number-crunching exercise rather than building and managing relationship with customers.

The study of customers' loyalty to a product or brand is not new. Perhaps, its beginning goes back to the time when marketing was not yet considered an established profession or academic discipline. Today, customer loyalty is often studied under brand management, so the name brand loyalty. This, therefore, has taken a different direction all together, leading to the study of such topics as the power of branding, image building and mind setting as well as other communication related areas. Branding strategy as practiced by firms and the level of academic studies carried out in this area cannot be ignored.

The topic that is not much talked about under CRM, however, is customer complaint behavior and complaint handling or resolution. Nevertheless, customer complaint behavior or CCB and complaint resolution (CR) process are gaining attention in the marketing literature today. Also, such issues are sometimes explored under Relationship Marketing (RM). Although RM focuses both on customer and employee relationships, the emphasis is mainly on customer employee satisfaction and the power of communication. One should appreciate the fact that customer loyalty, CRM, CCB and complaint resolution are all interlinked. In the meantime, it is necessary to look customer loyalty from a different perspective. Ideally, it should be customer product loyalty rather than brand loyalty.

It is, in fact, fair to say that brand loyalty is something psychological and of an attachment or affinity driven by emotions directed at the brand rather than the product itself. But in reality, it is the product and not the brand that gives the customer the value and benefit (mostly tangible). Brand itself is an intangible attachment to the 'product package' created to facilitate communication between the firm and the customer. Brand by itself does not have any value to the customer other than some psychological benefits but it helps communicate the values and attributes of the product. When the product performs and delivers as expected, the attached brand name accumulates goodwill and creates a positive image. But, when it fails to perform, the opposite is true.

Similarly, the same thing is true with corporate reputation. The company itself has a brand identity, and sometimes, it is the same as the product brand name. In this case, a negative brand image can hurt the corporate reputation and vise versa. If the company has a separate brand identity, then company reputation can be at stake due to several other causes such as corporate philosophy regarding its commitment to environment, corporate social responsibility (CSR), and quality & customer satisfaction. Such corporate philosophy is often tested in the market place by the firm's promise and commitment as well as by the actions the firm takes to resolve the crisis or problem as it emerges. Therefore, it is essential to note that someone's loyalty behavior toward a product or brand name is also linked to his or her loyalty towards the firm's band image or corporate reputation

Customer Brand Loyalty Curve

Customer Brand Loyalty should not be confused with customer life-cycle or customer relationship cycle that often describes the progression of steps a customer goes through over a period of time. Such steps may be consideration, purchase, use, and building loyalty etc. Here the brand loyalty is the last step in the curve. In the meantime, customer behavior indeed would change over a period of time that can have implications for product or brand performance. On the other hand, brand loyalty curve starts with the time when the customer begins to flirt with the brand before a relationship emerges.

Here the author considers customer brand loyalty as a behavior that is packaged as a product and attempts to explore its trends over a period of time. In doing so, customer loyalty behavior or CLB to products and brands will be treated mainly but CLB to companies and its impacts of corporate reputation will also be examined briefly. It is claimed that the relationship between customer loyalty to a brand (or firm) name and the time factor is said to show three distinct phases unless it is prematurely broken. These three phases, plotted as a curve as in product life cycle, are development or loyalty building stage, reinforcement or loyalty continuity stage, and decline or disloyalty stage.

The entry at the beginning and exit at the end of the cycle are also obviously important but to be treated separately. The size (determined by the intensity of loyalty and the amount of time) of the customer Loyalty Life Cycle (LLC) curve can vary depending on the type of customer or type of product involved. The LLC of a product for two different segments of the market can also be different. Similarly, the LLC of two different products involving one specific customer segment are also different.

However, the intensity of loyalty and the time factor are relative determinants. For some products, the time period can be two to three years or more and for others, it can be as short as a few months. Also, market segments as determined by traditional methods based on demographic, geographic, or cultural factors may seem deceiving when it comes to plotting the LLC for a product. In the IT-driven age of Internet, market segmentations needs to assume some innovative variables such as those factors that determine the level of brand loyalty.

It is believed that LLC curves of a specific market segment can be constructed for a product or brand in question when the market segment is clearly identified and their loyalty behavior (aggregate intensity of a sample of customers) is determined. It is important here to determine an innovative market or customer segmentation method where a group of customers can be identified based on the similarity or homogeneity of their brand loyalty behavior.

From the product perspective, it is important to consider the issues of brand dilution due to brand extension and co-branding or product extension to include other products (or a line of products) under a specific brand name. Moreover, the influence of corporate image and reputation on the product or a brand under investigation should also be taken into consideration. As we have noted before, in some cases, the product and corporate brand name can be the same.

In this book, the author attempts to examine first the concept of customer brand loyalty from a number of perspectives. The key assumption is that the loyalty is both behavioral attributes and a marketable product offered by the customer. When the behavioral attributes are packaged and exchanged as a loyalty product, customers would expect something in return in addition to the actual goods they buy. Could it be reciprocal loyalty?

Major part of the book is about customer brand loyalty management. This involves building, retaining, protecting and restoring brand loyalty strategically. This is again aimed at recruiting and retaining customers. Having developed a strategic framework for the management of loyalty, author examines and discusses the analytical process and techniques that are involved in assessing the perceived level of customer loyalty as well as companies' efforts to built and manage it. The third part of the book deals with setting goals and objectives and strategies for managing customer loyalty. The last part of the book examines the various strategies or Customer Loyalty Management (CLM) programs that may be available for companies to choose from in order to achieve the brand loyalty goals and objectives.

2 Customer Brand Loyalty-Behavioral Attributes Packaged as a Product

Loyalty Behavior Defined

People often develop and express loyalty behavior and attachments among other people and organizations in various occasions. Outside parents and siblings, loyalty and attachment can be commonly found between friends, spouses (or partners), employees and organization (or company and boss). Whatever it may be, loyalty perhaps, could be defined as a bond built by trust and expectation. For example, a relationship called friendship between two individuals can develop and reach the stage of maturity and then lead to decline over a period of time when trust and commitment from either party go through growth to decline. In most cases, it can also terminate abruptly and prematurely when confidence and trust cease to exist between friends.

This is also the case of relationship between spouses or life-partners. Whether committed by an oath or not, partners can end up in separation or divorce when their relationship terminates because of declining trust and commitment (loyalty). Sometimes the separation can be sudden and premature, and occasionally, it can even happen after years of co-habitation due to gradual decline in loyalty.

Another common form of loyalty that is often talked about is between an employee and an organization. Employees are often expected to show loyalty to their organizations. But today, the world is full of uncertainty and gone are the days when employees were expected to be loyal to their employers. In tribal societies of Africa or even some middle-eastern or west-Asian countries, people still remain loyal to their tribal chief or Aga as in the feudal system but it is declining fast.

Whatever may be the form of loyalty that people develop between each other; there exists an element of emotion here. Such emotions, when expressed between people and things such as products and customer, are not the same as in the case of two individuals. However, by building a positive relationship between the customer and the organization (technically the people or employees and staff in the organization who are normally referred to as the Brand Representatives), some degree of emotion in loyalty can be brought back.

This also becomes possible by branding the product and linking the product attributes and benefits to the brand name and the image thus created. It can be the same in the case of employees and an organization such as a company. If the management (or the owner) and the staff can establish a good relationship between them, then the bond and trust as well the loyalty between the two parties can become stronger. Similarly, a political party can attract loyalty from members via strong relationships between the party leadership and the members. Nevertheless, what is important is the difference between customer loyalty to a product or brand and the loyalty that is found between two individuals.

Factors that may Influence Loyalty Behavior

The next question is what factors can help develop loyalty between individuals. For example, loyalty between friends or spouses may depend on several factors such as the matching qualities and attributes, including similar goals and common interests. Moreover, both parties may need to build confidence in each other by successful experiences. It also means, showing commitments to help each other directly or indirectly, when needed. In other words, there should be some degree of satisfaction by being loyal to each other because both seem to have had some expectations. Nevertheless, problems in relationship can occur because of misunderstanding and lack of communication or its ineffectiveness. Therefore, if a relationship between two individuals exist and then loyalty is to be built, the above noted attributes need to be communicated effectively too.

The 'product' under consideration here is the 'relationship' between two friends or spouses. The loyalty factor is said to exist between two individuals through a product called relationship. In other words, individuals whether friends or spouses, should express their loyalty through trustworthy relationships and when the relationship is spoiled, loyalty between friends or spouses decline and could come to an end when it becomes untenable. Sign of disloyalty means broken relationship.

Building relationship and loyalty between two individuals, therefore, is not all that easy and simple. The attributes of relationship and loyalty discussed above may be demanding so much from each other that the partners would have to undergo several painful experiences before they could claim to have built a solid relationship. In the meantime, accepting someone for a relationship or the 'entry' stage may well be an accidental event or even by careful search as well as planned and well intended to help satisfy one's own expectation. Moreover, the entry stage could also be costly requiring parties to spend time and other resources. It may also be the right time and place that prompted the entry stage of a relationship. Lastly, one or both would have to make some effort and promote each other before entering into a relationship. During the entry as well as at the initial stages of a relationship, both individuals will have to 'flirt' with loyalty. This remains the early stage of building loyalty.

At the early stage, suspicions are easily overcome by hope and thereby keeping the promises and confirming to the implicit rules and building confidence in each other. This can be accompanied by strong commitments to friendship while communicating effectively so that both individuals could successfully build a relationship and reinforce their loyalty to each other. The exit stage is characterized by having severe breakdown in relationship. A few failures such as not keeping up to the promise, intentionally or unintentionally showing no interests to each others cause, and apparent lack of commitment such as not being available when needed are all sings of slipping loyalty. At this stage, there is no motivation at all to 'restore' the failing relationship other than just waiting for an opportunity to exit. This is the stage of apathy and disengagement. When such an opportunity arises, either partner may break the bond and exit.

One may wonder if the same analogy could be used to explain the relationship between a customer and an organization (organization can be commercial or non-profit such an educational institution). The answer is obvious. In CRM, it is the relationship between customer and the company that is being managed, and not the relationship between a product or brand and the customer. This argument becomes crystal clear when the product sold happened to be a 'service' because service is rather intangible and that is produced and consumed concurrently, therefore, perished instantly. However, through successful service experiences, managers can still establish and sustain good relationships between customers and the service companies. The whole argument may, however, raise the question whether companies should pay attention to corporate reputation and image as much as the brand image of the product when developing and promoting customer loyalty. Obviously, corporate reputation of a service organization becomes crucial in this regard.

A relationship can indeed exist between a customer and a company because of the product that the company manufactures or sell to the customer. But it is often unconceivable that such a relationship can exist between the product and the customer. Of course the customer can develop an affinity, dependence, and trust as well as loyalty through its brand name. Therefore, the concept of relationship management essentially means managing relationship between customers and a company (technically between people in the company). This becomes more evident in the case of business to business (B2B) relationship as well as in service organizations.

Brand names of products and companies become an integral part of the product by which the customer tries to create an image and perception about them. The customer through the brand name perceives all those attributes of relationship such as trust and dependability and therefore customer loyalty towards a product is often reflected in its brand name and image. The concept of integrated loyalty, therefore, is said to include all aspects of customer loyalty; loyalty to product, loyalty to the company that produced it, company that sold it, as well as the brand names associated with the product and company.

Marketing literature in the meantime identifies two dimensions of customer loyalty. The true loyalty that is driven by trust and confidence coupled with emotions is called attitudinal loyalty while the action-driven events such as repeat purchase is called behavioral loyalty. The former may lead to establish the later but there may be other factors also that can cause the latter. Convenience, value for money, lack of similar products or substitute products nearby, and even existing membership to loyalty programs such as the frequent-flyer schemes are some of the reasons that one may happen to be a repeat customer.

However, the concept of customer loyalty seems more complex than that can be explained by one's attitude and behavior towards a brand and company image. Moreover, even if customer brand loyalty is to be defined by these two dimensions, it needs to be integrated and combined together if the magnitude and intensity of loyalty are to be assessed. Product benefits and attributes, convenience and product availability, sales promotion and price-value factor, and perceived brand image and company reputation are all important factors that may lead to behavioral loyalty. Similarly, promise and expectation (company-customer); confidence and trust; commitment and customer satisfaction; and communication and reinforcement are factors that may shape up customer attitudes that lead to attitudinal loyalty.

Here, by integrating and cross matching these variables, some concrete loyalty determinants can be established. This also means, both the company and the customer need to be merged. Firms cannot expect customers to be simply loyal when the firm is not. Customer loyalty to brands therefore comes from company's loyalty to its customers. Businesses should therefore show commitment and establish loyalty towards their customers. It's a mutual process as between two individuals and if the organization (firm) itself cannot establish this loyalty, then it should be established by product branding strategies. True loyalty is like a love affair between two individuals and each would do their best not to disappoint the other. Once the customer is emotionally trapped, as when it is in the maturity or continuity stage of the loyalty life cycle, it is difficult to break up the love affair.

Brand Loyalty Defined as a Product

In the introductory chapter, we have already seen loyalty as something offered for sale by the customers. It means loyalty costs money. In the normal exchange process between the buyer and seller, it is about the goods and services that would satisfy customer needs and wants and money that represent the cost and profit for the seller.

Here, the product called 'loyalty' represents something that is separate from these exchanges and does not involve any financial transactions between the buyer and seller. Of course, the seller of this product called loyalty is the traditional customer and the buyer or receiver is the firm that offers the product. So, what does the firm or buyer gives back in return to acquire the product called 'loyalty' from customer? It is again a reciprocal loyalty product. In order to simplify this concept, let's call the sellers' (customer) loyalty as 'Customer Loyalty' and the buyers' (company) loyalty as 'Reciprocal Loyalty'. This exchange between the customer and firm or producer is therefore the reverse process where the latter attempts to woo the formers' loyalty by offering reciprocal loyalty. In many instances, it is a long-term process accompanied by tens if not hundreds of normal exchanges and transactions involving goods & services and money.

The author believes that customer loyalty is explained and measured by benefit-centered, value-centered, convenience-centered and image-centered behaviors based on loyalty determining factors such as conformity, confidence, commitment and communication (four Cs). Reciprocal loyalty is determined by the product attributes such as benefits, value, convenience, and image that are offered by the brand or firm according to the criteria defined by the four Cs. As a product package, loyalty itself has several components: the core, secondary and augmented product components. When a firm is trying to buy loyalty from a customer, the core component of the product is something of an emotional attachment through affinity and bonding to a specific brand. If this attachment is to be effective, it should lead to an action (or behavior) called 'purchase'. But one could always have an attachment and affinity to a brand without culminating in any purchase. Also, a purchase episode could be a regular and consistent event or irregular occasional event.

The secondary product component of loyalty is something of an additional affinity towards a product or brand as shown by the customer. For example, customer loyalty may extend to reach out for the product or brand even in unusual and unexpected circumstances. The third component, augmented product is considered an additional bonanza for the firm. The customer here may even extend to reach out and promote the product or brand to friends and family members through word-of-mouth advertising. This is something like the 'inspirational customer' or evangelists for their favorite brands as Kevin Roberts described in his book, LOVEMARK.

The reciprocal loyalty, on the other hand, is said to have shown by the firm towards its customers. As perceived by the customer, the core product component of this loyalty is company's sincere commitment to offer the core attribute as promised implicitly or explicitly and therefore sought and expected by the customers. A core attribute can be one of the four attributes of benefit, value, convenience, and image but often it is the benefit attributes. Firm's commitment to offer the core attributes should lead to actual performance and delivery so that an equal exchange between customer loyalty and reciprocal loyalty can take place. The secondary component of reciprocal loyalty product is the secondary attributes that are sought by the customer and often promised by the firm to deliver. In general, such attributes can be value and convenience attributes. The third and the augmented product components are often the last attributes of image that is primarily psychological in characteristics.

3 Brand Loyalty Life-cycle and Loyalty Matrix

Brand Loyalty Life Cycle

Having defined the 'loyalty behavior' of customers, it becomes relatively easy to understand the nature and characteristics of the brand loyalty curve or BLC. The BLC has been already defined as the relationship between the intensity (magnitude) of loyalty and the time factor. In other words, it is the graphic representation of customer loyalty behavior to a brand (or company) over a period of time (intensity as the dependent variable in Y axis and time in either months or years as the independent variable in X axis). Earlier, it was postulated that the BLC has a product life cycle with three distinct stages.

The initial stage is represented by a growth curve sloping up and the peak by a maturity stage consisting of a rather flat or horizontal curve and the last stage with a downward slope of decline in loyalty intensity. The real challenge here is to determine the level of intensity of customer brand loyalty first. Measuring the intensity of loyalty in quantitative terms is rather difficult and requires us to identify and construct certain appropriate instruments.

The instruments to be used should also reflect the aggregate intensity of loyalty (loyalty behavior) rather than just the loyalty behavior based on a single attribute. The product brand image and the corporate image as well as the firm's reputation are also important. Once the customers of the product or company and or both are identified, then focus group interview technique or even survey questionnaire can be employed to rate the level of the intensity of brand loyalty. The major problem, however, is the issues of individual versus group loyalty.

Every brand in the market may have thousands or hundreds of thousand customers and it is not practical and logical to establish their loyalty level to a brand or company individually. Therefore, it is essential to identify a handful of groups or segments consisting of homogeneous customers with similar brand loyalty behavior. This leads us to consider market segmentation based on loyalty attributes. Before CLB-led customer (or market segmentation) segmentation is examined, it is also important to look at other related issues of loyalty attributes and their significances using the concept of Brand Loyalty Matrix. Brand loyalty matrix is the product of cross-tabulation of two variables. On the X-axis is the 'degree of brand and or product differentiation' caused by the loyalty-driven attributes provided. The Y-axis represents the 'significance of these differentiations as perceived by the customer'. The additional attributes provided may be just single or multiple factors and are often benefit, value or convenience as well as image-based attributes.

Customer Brand Loyalty Matrix

	A	B
Significance of Attribute as Perceived by the Customers	High	High degree of Differentiation and perceived Significance
	D	C
	Low	High

Degree of Differentiation

Here, the four boxes (A, B, C, and D clockwise from upper left-hand corner) represent four levels of customer brand loyalty that can be expected. In quadrant A, the perceived significance of the loyalty attribute or attributes that are offered to differentiate the brand is very high. But the degree of differentiation offered is very low. Perhaps, the attributes offered may be just one item or slightly different from the original version. For example, if the product brand is a cell phone and the extra attribute offered is just color image. Or, perhaps, the attribute offered is simply the reduction in price. Being a relatively good brand, the brand now not only offers some differentiation but also some benefits which indeed make a case for increased affinity for some segments of the target market.

The attributes used to differentiate the product here are rather invisible: may be a single attribute or, perhaps, they are not effectively communicated to the customers in order to make the difference. Usually service elements are added as secondary products to the core or primary product or benefit in order to differentiate the product features. Even with a single attribute, products can be differentiated effectively if additional features are added to the core product or benefit. In any case, the differentiation here is highly significant as perceived by the customer. In reality, these customers are from existing target market. In order to retain these customers' loyalty, companies should carefully evaluate the attributes that could make the differentiation highly significant.

The customer loyalty to brands in quadrant A is moderate to low and the required company strategy would be aimed at moving the level of differentiation from the existing level to a higher level. This may require adding some visible attributes or features to the brand. These additions may be either in the form of secondary products or even an effective communication method to inform the existing attributes that are used for differentiation (strong brand image). The objective is to move the brand from quadrant A to quadrant B.

In quadrant B, the brand attributes are highly differentiated, both in the features of core and secondary products. Most likely, there are multiple attributes. Even if the attributes provided for differentiation are not exceptionally different from those of competitors', its brand image and perception can be very powerful that would make a difference in the mind of the target and potential customers. Here the target customers, mainly the existing customers would love it and continue to show loyalty as long as the company continues to provide the attributes expected.

What is important is to pay careful attention to the vital attributes as described by benefit, value, convenience, and image that would help the existing target market identify and differentiate the product features as different from those of competitors' so that a match can be made to love each other (customer and the brand name). Here the company objective should be aimed at retaining the products in the B quadrant. Therefore the strategy would be to continue to offer the same level of differentiation. This should be accompanied by consistent communication campaigns in order to retain the existing customer perception on the significance of differentiation. Of course, the attributes provided should also offer the benefits expected so that the customer perception remains positive.

The third quadrant, C, is an interesting quadrant in which the product brand is highly differentiated as in B, but the target customers are potential customers who do not perceive the attributes (used for differentiation) as highly significant. Also, some of the customers are among the existing target market that would not perceive the differentiated brand attributes as highly significant. Another possible reason could be not having a powerful brand image or lack of an effective communication strategy to inform the customers about the significance of attributes. The target customers of this quadrant, as in quadrant A whose loyalty is low, are most likely to float in-between and switch brand easily.

Because of the high degree of differentiation of products in quadrant C, the cost of the product may seem to be higher than those of quadrant A. The objective for the company here is to move the customers from quadrant C to B by raising the level of perceived significance of the brand attributes. The firm may have two options here. First is to identify those attributes that are not considered significantly important and remove them from the offering. Secondly, the firm can develop a powerful communication strategy to inform and raise the level of perceived significance among the existing customers.

The last quadrant D is characterized by having low level of perceived significance and low degree of product or brand differentiation. As far as the products of this quadrant are concerned, they are essential goods and services. Even if they are slightly differentiated with extra attributes, customer does not see them as important. Customer brand loyalty here is the lowest among all products. However, some of the customers from the target consumers of these products can be wooed to be loyal by providing some secondary product attributes at no cost or lowest possible cost to the customers. The existing customers are also customers of other brands or sellers such as a baker for whose product nobody would show loyalty. Most often, such products are generic or non-branded goods and or difficult to differentiate.

The objective of the company or seller here is to move the customer from this quadrant to any other quadrant, preferably to A which is cheaper because no need for providing tangible attributes but perceived significance through some service elements used for a low degree of differentiation. Branding and advertisements can also create customer perceptions leading to moving the customers to the A quadrant. If it seems feasible, companies can also try to differentiate their products by adding some intangible attributes such as home delivery and move the products to category C or B.

Overall Strategy for Customer Loyalty Improvement

The loyalty matrix helps us to determine and evaluate the loyalty levels of certain customer groups to a range of products. The four quadrants: A, B, C, and D are defined by the product brand characteristics as offered by the seller or manufacturer and as seen by the customer. Here, the brands in the B quadrants are said to have the potential for enjoying the highest level of customer loyalty. While the brands in quadrants A and C are said to fetch moderate level of loyalty, those in the D quadrant are said to receive the lowest level of loyalty or no loyalty.

Therefore, by loyalty improvement, it is meant that the brand needs to be moved to the B quadrant from both A and C quadrants. Also, it is about moving the product or brand from quadrant D to any other quadrant. In this process, the magnitude of the variables in the X-axis and Y-axis need to increase. If the brand is not differentiated, companies may want to consider adding tangible and intangible attributes. Such attributes may be product improvement, extra features with additional benefits, and value enhancement for the customers, and convenience to customers when it comes to purchasing, and branding and image creation. In the end, it is also necessary to inform effectively and convince the customer that the extra attributes provided have some significance.

This process is rather difficult and often accompanied by educating the customer over a long period of time. It is also important to realize that some of the extra attributes offered for differentiation do not seem to have any benefits or value for some customers and they would not perceive the attributes as having any significance. Therefore attempt should be made to identify the right attributes to be added so that a match can be made to customer needs and wants. An effective communication strategy, in any case, would play an important role in helping the customer identify the hidden needs and wants and in informing the customer about them. This is what most of the effective advertisement campaigns would be expected to deliver.

Loyalty Behavior and CLB-led Market Segmentation

Common loyalty behavior among customers if and when tracked and grouped can become the basis for effective market segmentation. The objective here is to segment the market based on customer loyalty behavior or CLB. It is essentially a process of converging customers to a homogeneous group of people whose loyalty behavior would show similarity. Therefore what determines loyalty behavior or what would cause the customers to express their loyalty to a product or brand becomes the focal point here.

What seems important is the determinants of loyalty behavior are also instruments that are used to measure the intensity or magnitude of loyalty. On the one hand, some of these determinants are used as segmentations variables. On the other hand, they can also be considered as the instruments by which the intensity of loyalty is measured. The challenge is therefore to identify such unique factors that can be used to achieve these two objectives. CLB-led market segmentation will be examined in detail in chapter 5. In the meantime, it is necessary to look at the determinants of customer brand loyalty behavior so that they can be matched with behavioral attributes.

4 Determinants of Loyalty Behavior and Loyalty Attributes

The Four plus One 'C' Variables

Technically speaking, it is fair to say that there are no true CLB studies can be found in the marketing literature, except for the already noted attitudinal and behavioral loyalty. While most researches focus on the power of branding on loyalty behavior and the role of loyalty (loyalty cards) programs in retaining customers, a handful of studies examine the causes of loyalty and other issues such as brand switching. Of course, there may be numerous reasons why a customer switches brands or even ditch a brand or company altogether. Brand (or product-service) failure in satisfying the customer, tarnishing brand image, non-availability of the branded product when needed, over-pricing, repeated breakdown in brand or product performance, lack of a framework for handling customer complaints, and even ineffective communication between the customers and the producer or supplier are some the most common reasons why anyone would switch a brand.

Based on an extensive examination of the marketing literature on consumer behavior and complaint behavior and CRM, as well as on branding, the author was able identify and categorize the causes and determinants of loyalty behavior as consisting four plus one 'C's. According to the author, these five Cs, in fact, refers to the company efforts and actions that are perceived as important by the customers in generating customer brand loyalty.

- **Conformity**: it refers to the specifications and standards of product-service provision as well as of post-purchase services, including complaints handling and conforming to those standards. In other wards, it technically refers to company's promise or assurance.

- **Confidence**: it means building customer confidence by being reliable for successful product-service outcomes or performance as well as successful resolution of customer complaints. This simply means being reliable and dependable in general and during product-service delivery.

- **Commitment**: this simply means commitment to excellence. Committing to provide customer satisfaction by going an extra mile to make the customer happy.

- **Communication**: it is about effectively communicating the above factors and providing appropriate and pertinent information to customers using various direct and indirect methods that are appropriate.

- **Continuity**: this is about consistency in providing the key attributes as described by the marketing mix variables: product benefits, value, convenience, and perception (product quality and improvement, value for money, efficient distribution and product availability as well as building and promoting a positive brand image and perception).

The first four of the 5Cs, conformity, confidence, commitment, and communication are considered company-driven factors that can be used to explain the causes of customer loyalty behavior. These factors are also rather strategic in nature requiring the company to plan and deliver on a long to medium term basis. The company also needs to be visionary and proactive in this regards. The last C, the continuity factor has two sides: the company-driven tactical factor that it needs to attend on a day-to-day basis and the customer-driven continuity factor that would help determine the CLB towards a brand (either product brand or company image).

Moreover, the first four Cs are akin to attitude building factors and the four marketing mix variables (attributes) of last C, continuity, are like the behavior related factors. While the last C or continuity factor that would help to determine the customer loyalty behavior towards the company or its products is said to involve micro managing the marketing mix variables, its role as the customer-driven attributes of CLB may have a slightly different meaning. In this regard, the continuity factor has four attribute determinants: product-driven attribute (benefit), price-driven attribute (value), place-driven attribute (convenience), and promotion-driven (image and reputation) attribute.

Conformity:

Companies always talk about product specifications and making products according to certain standards. Some of the standards are driven by customer expectation and companies' effort to gain competitive advantage over rival firms. Firms, in the meantime, could establish their own product-service standards (benchmarking), quality assurance policies and programs, and other performance standards. Today many firms attempt to acquire ISO quality certifications for both production and delivery of products and services as well as for the process of production and delivery.

Today's sophisticated customers understand these standards much more than ever before. Also, companies make promises to deliver quality and standards to customers either intentionally or because of consumer pressure or even due to competition. When the product-service keeps performing as expected, customers begin to show affinity towards these products or brands and their producers. Here, product-service failure may seem less frequent and company commits itself to deliver its promises. This is what conformity means, conforming to the set standards and keeping its promises. The conformity factor mainly focuses on the responsibility of the company that produces the product or that sells the product (or brand) as a retailer. Moreover, conformity also means the measures that the company takes to implement conformity policies and programs as well as to deal with the post-purchase services, including complaints resolution. The following can be considered as some of the indicating criteria that would satisfy the conformity determinant:

- A company or organization having well-documented product and service specifications.

- A company or organization having clear and well-defined mission statement, goals and objectives as well as policies regarding production and service delivery process and customer relations as well as customer satisfaction.

- Commitment to product service quality via quality assurance programs and implementation plans. Or having ISO certifications and or national standards certifications.

- Companies having policies regarding CRM and post-purchase services such as refunds; exchanges; maintenance; and customer complaints resolution: mechanism to encourage and facilitate complaints as well as effective complaints handling procedures.

- Service firms or organizations having proven service design and blueprints that would help enhance the service delivery and detect service fail points.

A firm may already have quality assurance programs and clear commitment to Total Quality Management (TQM). A well-documented product-service specification of both input resources and finished goods and services, benchmarking for further improvement, quality control system to measure and evaluate the variations are all related to the conformity factor.

The conformity factor provides the customer with assurance and guarantee about the quality of the product or brand and creates confidence on the company that produces and or sells the goods. This in fact provides an opportunity for the customer to generate trust and affinity as well as dependability leading to building loyalty eventually. Also, conformity factor plays an important role in attracting customers in the first place at the entry level of loyalty behavior curve. Brand names of the products and companies help to identify and communicate with the customers the contents of the conformity factor.

In a relationship between two individuals such as friends or spouses, the conformity factor involves the possession of consistent qualities and behavior patterns. This makes the relationship much more predictable and dependable and such qualities make individuals attract each other in the first place. Dependability and predictability also come from personality traits such as integrity and good character.

Confidence:

This is about helping the customers build confidence on the product or brand performance and the company by being reliable. Confidence comes from repeated successful outcomes when the customer flirts with the brand or company. Successful outcome means the product or the brand delivers what it is supposed to deliver. The product-service specifications described above and the performance standards promised as well as brand attributes as expected by the customer should prove highly satisfactory once the product is bought and consumed. If a digital camera is designed to work robustly in any condition, it should function even in an extremely cold climate. Similarly, if a fast food restaurant promises to serve customers in five minutes, it should deliver its promise when the customer expects to do so. In other words, the key word is reliability or dependability.

Successful outcomes also mean delivering quality as promised or implied. In the absence of any promised standards, it simply means generally accepted norms. For example, successful outcomes of a one-hour dry cleaning service should be that the garment is cleaned aesthetically, hygienically, and free from dirt & stains or particles as well as any odor. Moreover, it should have been cleaned using water-free solvent-based cleaning products and delivered in one hour as promised.

Confidence of customers also depends very much on how the company receives complaints and how it handles and resolves the complaints. The most important ingredient of CRM is building confidence on the company. Since most customers remain passive and fail to complain even when things go wrong, it is extremely vital to encourage and facilitate complaint behavior among customers. But, most importantly, when the customer complaints, the firm should act immediately and effectively to resolve the complaints successfully if the customer is to build confidence and loyalty. Repeated breakdown in product performance and failure to deliver as promised when customer complains would leads to ending the love affair between the customer and brand as well as the company prematurely. In a nutshell, the following can be said to have relevance to the confidence factor:

- Companies having effective program implementation (for quality assurance, CRM, and complaint resolution etc.) strategies with particular attention paid to resource allocation accompanied by timely and objective monitoring and evaluation programs in place (this also would be part of the conformity determinant).

- Adopting concepts and techniques such as Total Quality Management TQM), Quality Function Deployment (QFD), robust and foolproof designing, as well as concurrent or simultaneous engineering, particularly in the service sector.

- Conducting on-the-spot monitoring and control programs to assess whether outcomes and performance are satisfactory and quality is delivered as promised. This would include also the application of benchmarking and quality control charts etc. to evaluate performance.

- Provision of facilities and resources to guarantee post-purchase customer services such as repair and maintenance operation closer to the customer.

- Companies having innovative programs to encourage and facilitate customer complaint behavior and adopting strategies to handle complaints effectively.

The objective here is to make sure that the customer never loses his or her confidence on the brand or product and the company that produces or sells. The cost of customer turnover at this point would be very high if the brand and or company fails repeatedly to deliver. On the contrary, every successful outcome reinforces the customer confidence on the product or brand and company and often it is reflected through the brand image and company goodwill. The flirting customer now is expected to fall in love with the brand.

Commitment:

Commitment factor has an extraordinary influence on the customer. When a company is committed to serve the customer, it makes customer satisfaction the number one priority. Obviously, the other two determinants discussed above, conformity and confidence factors, pave the way for customer orientation in a company. But when it commits to make an extra effort to satisfy the customer, it touches deep in the heart of the customer. Such a commitment is more than just a commitment to excel in quality.

A company can manifest its commitment to deliver customer satisfaction in all three stages of the customer buying process. When the staff makes an extra effort to give pertinent information about the product specifications or post-purchase services during the pre-purchase stage, potential customers can be easily wooed into buying the product. Any extra effort made by the staff to make the customer comfortable during the purchasing time would also make the customer extremely satisfied. Similarly, when the customer is treated well with courtesy and dignity during the post-purchase stage, including the time of complaint handling, customer would never fail to express their loyalty.

Company's commitment to deliver the best takes place first in the back of the house. Whether in the assembly line of an automobile factory or in the kitchen of a fine dining restaurant, it is the employees and the management commitment and effort to achieve the best possible result, and sometime, to surpass the standards of optimum level that brings about commitment. It means, never make room for any errors. Effective management of the supply chain becomes vital here. Obviously, it may involve the supply network outside, including those of outsourced and the internal supply chains with the organization or company. For example, quality of the raw material used matters as much as the quality of production itself.

Secondly, it is the commitment to maintain the set standards or surpass the best level during the sales stage or service delivery stage in the service sector. This may requires the cooperation of several other organizations such as the distribution and retail firms. Sometimes, customers' affinity and loyalty to a brand can diminish because of the tarnished reputation of the retailer. Here, the focus is on customer service characterized by courtesy and respect, attentiveness, patience, helpfulness, and honesty of the staff. These qualities cannot be replaced by technology and therefore requires employee participation with a human touch.

An extra effort that the staff takes to make the customer happy can bring about miracles in generating customer loyalty. Commitment also meant the extraordinary effort that a company makes to satisfy the customer during the post-purchase stage. This is where the customer may have to complain about the product performance or company's failure to deliver as promised. The customer service approach and the qualities described above are also important here. Most firms fail in delivering customer service. This can happen even if the firm has established customer service policies but no commitment to deliver.

The following points can be summarized as having relevance to the commitment factor in general:

- Companies committing to implement policies and programs that are meant to guarantee established product service specifications as well as quality.

- Effective management of the supply chain network, both external and internal. It also means commitment to assure the quality of input resources, monitoring the standards of the outsourced services and the effectiveness of the operating systems.

- Commitment to serve the customer and deliver the products with the highest degree of customer satisfaction during the exchange and transaction processes.

- Ensuring and providing measures to train and educate the sales staff in order to serve the customer with dignity, respect, courtesy, attentiveness, and honesty as well as being helpful to customers whenever asked for during the purchase process.

- Companies committing to deliver the best after-sale services, including when complaints are received and resolved effectively to the satisfaction of the customers.

- Companies enabling to build a corporate culture where the management and staff take an extra effort to make the customer feel better and satisfied.

Commitment factor can be well defined as the honest effort that the companies take to serve the customer well above the expected norms, no matter at what stage the customer is being served. It is important to recognize the three stages when customers expect such commitments from companies. Obviously, they are the pre-purchase stage, purchase stage and post-purchase stage.

Communication:

Communication remains one of the most important factors in any kind of relationship. Even in person-to-person communication, it can take several forms. Communication does not mean just informing or delivering a message. The content of the message, style with which it is delivered, objective and the medium of the communication are all important. Here, the communication factor is about effectively informing and convincing the customer mainly on the first three loyalty determinants.

The companies often explicitly guarantee appropriate product-service specifications, and promise to deliver the best quality. In the first place, the customer should feel and see the entire communication effort credible; message and content, media used, and delivery method. The message should also be delivered convincingly that the customers could trust the company to deliver what it promises. Also, the message is about building confidence during the time of purchase.

Secondly, customer should be assured that measures have been taken to deliver the product and services as promised and all necessary resources and facilities are in place. Moreover, customer should be informed that the company welcomes feedback and complaints when things are not delivered as promised. It is also necessary to inform the customer unambiguously how the complaints will be resolved and what would be the firm's policies regarding refunds, exchanges and replacements.

The third message is about and linked to the commitment factor. Communicating to the customer about company's commitment to deliver customer satisfaction should appear honest and convincing. Here, the message content, media used, and how and when it is delivered is all extremely important. Because the customer service aspect and the human factor associated with it make the communication process rather different and difficult. Here, often the medium of communication is company employees and staff and the forms of communication are not just verbal. In a nutshell, the following points can be considered as relevant to the communication factor.

- Effective communication remains one of the vital tools that can help inform and convince the customer about other loyalty determinants such as conformity, confidence, and commitment.

- Communication is not just sending message and informing. To be effective and convincing, companies should carefully evaluate the communication objectives, media, forms, and the audience.

- Every loyalty determinant or factor noted so far requires different communication strategy. Contents of the conformity factor should be clearly and easily understandable (example: product specifications and standards) and the after-sales and CRM policies should be clear and convincing. Written form of communication may be more suitable.

- For the confidence factor, communication objective should be directed at clearing misunderstanding and the medium is essentially the service staff of the company.

- Similarly, the commitment factor requires the communication medium to be company staff where the human factor plays an important role when it comes to expressing honesty, courtesy or attentiveness etc. that would enhance customer satisfaction.

If a company wishes to enhance customer loyalty by means of conformity, confidence, and commitment factors, communication remains the key factor that can help achieve this objective. No matter how good a company conforms to its standards and promises; how well it helps build confidence among customers; and how real its commitment to serve the customer, without effective and convincing communication, company would not satisfactorily achieve its objective of loyalty enhancement.

Continuity Factor and Loyalty Attributes

Continuity is the last factor that is said to determine customer loyalty. Unlike the other four determinants, continuity plays a unique role in boosting the loyalty behavior after all it is a customer behavior-driven line function. That means its role is rather tactical when it comes to managing the loyalty curve. In doing so, the company is expected to micro-manage the four marketing mix variables almost on a day-to-day basis. The critical issues that are related to the product mix are clear. All said and done about product quality and specifications under the conformity factor should be seen by the customer as true and deliverable in reality. In other words, the company should continue to offer the expected product or brand benefits (i.e. the product or brand attributes and promised benefits). Also, customer should be able to relate to the product or brand attributes (primary and secondary) and its benefits.

The product attributes should speak loudly about the perceived brand image that the firm has created in the customers mind. And, of course, this image has to continue. In this respect, the second aspect of the product mix is innovation and continuous product improvement. Due to changing customer expectations and competition, as well as to assure consistency, the firm is forced to improve the product or brand attributes and quality continuously.

The second continuity variable is related to price attribute of the product or brand, and therefore, value for money as perceived by the customer. Does the brand continue to provide the perceived value in terms of its benefits for the price that customer pays? Customers' assessment of brand or product value based on the price versus quality or in terms of the benefits that it provides is a complex process, which the firms may find difficult to understand. Pricing should not be based just only on the cost factor and the elasticity of demand. There may be other customer-driven factors such as perceived quality and therefore justifiable higher price.

Whatever the circumstances maybe, compulsory price increase may have to be justified and communicated effectively if customer loyalty is to be restored and retained. Many would attempt to switch brands at least temporarily when a price increase comes as a surprise and it often occurs unexpectedly without an advance warning. When a price increase is accompanied by product improvement and added brand value, then it is advisable to offer the new product as an alternative choice first before removing the old product from the shelf.

The place attribute or availability is the third continuity variable. One aspect of the place variable is the location of the business such as a hotel, bank or any retail outlets. The other aspect is the availability of the product when and where the customer needs it. The company needs to make sure that the channels of distribution and logistics are effectively functioning and the product availability is assured at all locations where the target customer would expect it. As in the case of price variable, most customers would try another brand if the product were not available when he or she needs it.

The last of the continuity variable is the promotion mix. The company is required to continue with its promotional programs so that the customer can be reminded about the brand and its promises; encouraged or induced by sales promotion; and informed about the changes that are taking place (product improvement, price increase, availability etc.). Companies can use appropriate methods and tools of promotion to achieve its objectives. Advertisement is an effective tool for informing and persuading the customer and sales promotion campaigns can really create values as some form of bonuses for the loyal customers. In addition, when in image crisis, public relations campaign would be essential in order to remedy the ruined image, and assure the continuity of the brand attributes and perceived quality.

Although the continuity factor (consisting of four variables as seen as above) can work in harmony with other factors, its use is very much tactical in nature. Also, sometimes, only one variable of the marketing or promotional mix such as sales promotion can be complemented for deficiency in another variable of the mix, say price increase.

5 CLB-led Market Segmentation

Customer Segmentation Based on Loyalty Behavior

A thorough examination of the determinants of loyalty behavior as discussed in the proceeding chapter would, indeed, help understand the Customer Loyalty Behavior (CLB) for a specific brand or company. Obviously, the CLB varies from brand to brand or even company to company. However, it is impossible to have a loyalty behavior curve established for every customer of a specific brand or company.

This is where the role of customer (market) segmentation comes in. However, in this day and age of electronic commerce and globalization, traditional methods of segmentation appear to become obsolete. Moreover, there are other issues to consider today. Increasing volume of services trade, growth of powerful electronic retailers such as the Amazon.com as well as retail platforms such as ebay and yahoo are creating the need for different branding strategy. For example, the loyalty factor lies more on the electronic retail platforms such as yahoo than the company that produces the product or brand to sell via medium.

It would seem appropriate to pay some attention here to the e-commerce market place in detail. Just imagine the famous platform such as Amazon as a product in itself within the concept of loyalty curve and the five determinants described above. It may seem a bit complicated but the loyalty factors here remain valid as in the case of any well-branded department store selling popular brands of various products. However, the IT-driven e-commerce platform is more prone to breakdown than the physical retail outlets. Partly, the blame may be on the customer's side for not being able to conform to the IT standards required to access the e-retailer. But where does the customer loyalty lie in this case? If the customers' IT system works trouble-free with another simple e-retailer platform, he or she may switch brand. Also, what about the intermediary of delivery firms such as the DHL or Royal Mail? Here, it is not the business to business delivery or distribution. Can the product brand image be ruined if the delivery firms did not keep its promise? Of the hundreds of thousands of books or parcels that the Amazon.com delivers every day, what percentage fails to meet customer expectations because of the failure of the distribution firm? So, where does the Amazon brand loyalty lies?

The level of loyalty as well as the crucial factors among the five Cs that determine loyalty behavior of a specific group of customers or market segment can, indeed, vary for different product classes. It can be different also for product versus services. So can be the case between traditional marketing and e-marketing, irrespective of the product or brand sold. In the meantime, loyalty behavior is also said to manifest by the type and level of strategic loyalty factors and tactical loyalty factors involved.

The strategic factors are the first four Cs of conformity, confidence, commitment, and communication (leading to form customer attitude) whereas the tactical factors are driven from the marketing mix variables of the last C, continuity (leading to customer behavior). However, these variables of product, price, place, and promotion are required to be labeled differently for the purpose of segmenting the market according to the framework suggested. The continuity variables are thus now named as 'benefit', 'value', 'convenience', and 'image' variables instead of product, price, place, and promotion.

The framework suggested here to segment the market based on the CLB also remains the first step towards quantifying and measuring the level or magnitude of customer brand loyalty. Here, the first four strategic Cs and the four tactical factors of the last C are used as variables in a matrix format for classification. The matrix as shown below consists of conformity, confidence, commitment, and communication as variables in the vertical column and benefits, value, convenience, and image in the horizontal row as the variables of continuity. For the sake of simplicity, the Customer Loyalty Behavior (CLB) is grouped into four categories and they are a) benefit-centered loyalty behavior, b) value-centered loyalty behavior, c) convenience-centered loyalty behavior, d) and image-centered loyalty behavior. The strategic factors that the company is supposed to use to respond to and assess these behaviors are conformity, confidence, commitment, and communication. These attribute variables are also used as criteria to develop instruments using the loyalty determinants in order to measure the level of CLB intensity later.

As for market segmentation, if the level of CLB intensity is appeared to be concentrated heavily in the 'benefit' column, then they are said to manifest benefit-centered loyalty behavior. The resulting market segment will be 'benefit-seeking' segment. Similarly, customers can be said to manifest other pattern such as value-centered, convenience-centered or image-centered behaviors if the loyalty intensity falls heavily on 'value' column, 'convenience' column, or image' column respectively. The respective market segments will be then value-seeking, convenience-seeking, and image-seeking segments.

Rationale for CLB-led Market Segmentation

The four market segmentation variables identified from the grid below are said to be universal in characteristic. In other wards, these Universal Market Segments or UMS can be applied for any market, irrespective of the product sold or the nature and type of firms participating in the market.

Table 1: Market (customer) Segmentation Grid

	Benefit	Value	Convenience	Image
C1*	guarantee of attributes, functionality, standards and quality	price stability policy and value for money assurance	promise of effective distribution channels and availability	assurance of prestige and exclusivity and positive brand image
C2*	delivering benefits as promised and successful outcome	delivering value for money and relative price stability	availability of product and in convenient locations	creating a brand image that is powerful and credible
C3*	going an extra mile to give the highest level of customer satisfaction	Making sincere effort to enhance value and benefits	availability of product even in Timbuktu when needed by customer	retaining and enhancing brand image & reputation
C4*	effectively Informing the above benefits to create added value	convincingly informing the price stability to generate perceived value and quality	effectively informing the customer about availability and service delivery locations	restoring & protecting brand image and firm's reputation. linking brand image to attributes

C1: Conformity, C2: Confidence, C3: Commitment C4: Communication

It is also suitable for the electronic market or the Internet market place. Although the four segmentation variables are derived from the well-known marketing mix variables, they have a behavioral connotation that is linked to customer loyalty. Therefore the variables have been given different names and as the names imply, these variables are more than just the marketing mix variables as we have known; product, price, place and promotion. Moreover, CLB-led market segmentation is superior to other traditional methods. This is because, whatever the geographic or demographic characteristics of customer, it is the behavior of the buyer leading to a successful purchase what matters the most to the marketer. Also, in this day and age of technology and Internet, geographic and demographic criteria are things of the past. Anybody could be living anywhere and purchasing anything. If there is a demand for a product or service, that would be bought. But what brand is bought, for how much it is bought, where it is bought, and when it is bought, all depend on the four factors described by the CLB attributes: benefit-seeking, value-seeking, convenience-seeking, and image-seeking behaviors.

Adoption of the free-market philosophy, coupled with ICT and other technological development as well as the sustaining income growth, enable the people all over the world to participate freely in the global purchasing exercise today. This shear force of globalization also breaks cultural barriers and social norms. Availability of globally branded products with effective and instant communication strategy worldwide makes the marketers wonder if and why the market needs to be segmented based on traditional segmentation characteristics.

Of course, one of the major objectives of market segmentation is to make the marketing function effective and efficient. It means producing the right product and targeting the right segment in order to optimize profit. In a diversified market characterized by having numerous demographic, social-cultural, and geographic traits, it is extremely difficult to attain these objectives. This, therefore, requires us to consider other more effective and logical approaches to market segmentation. And, nothing is more logical and effective than the proposed CLB-led approach.

Advantages of CLB-led Market Segmentation

The market segmentation method based on the customer brand loyalty behavior has a number of advantages over the traditional methods. Most importantly, the CLB-led segmentation is directly linked to determining customer purchase decisions. These decisions are obviously explained by a) benefits and attributes expected by the customer, b) value of the product as perceived by the customer, c) degree of convenience sought by the customer, and d) nature and type of perception or image generated in customer's mind.

In the case of market segmentation based on, for example, demographic criteria such as the age or income, it is difficult to determine the purchase behavior of an individual customer or group of customers. How can one predict that all middle-aged northerners prefer the taste of BODDINGTON or upper-middle income Californians would like to go to Hawaii for vacation?

Another advantage of the CLB-led segmentation method is its universality. It means it can be applied to all products and services irrespective of their characteristics. Particularly, this has relevance to the segmentation of business-to-business market where such criteria as the demographic variable do not seem to be useful. Therefore, whatever the type of market, whether industrial; consumer; or professional services, CLB-led segmentation method can be applied effectively in all cases.

Moreover, the growth of e-commerce and Internet marketing is another concern for the traditional marketer where the existing methods of segmentation seem inadequate. Irrespective of the demographic profile of the e-customers or their geographic locations, marketers can determine which CLB-led market segment that they would belong to relatively easily. Here, the loyalty-led behaviors discussed above (benefit-driven, value-driven, convenience-driven, and image-driven behaviors) are obviously linked to and judged by criteria such as conformity and expectation, confidence and reliability, commitment and satisfaction, and communication and perception.

Another advantage is, of course, that it can also be cross-linked with traditional segmentation variables such as the age or education level and occupation, if deemed necessary, for micro-segmentation. Moreover, according to the matrix table of loyalty-led criteria and behavior-driven variables shown in the grid above, there are sixteen micro market segments that the marketer can fine-tune to. Customers of a specific brand or company, however, would not be scattered around all the sixteen market segments identified here. What is important is to identify those few segments in which most of the customers would belong to. Since these factors identified are also loyalty-behavior determinants, they can also be used to measure the intensity of customer brand loyalty as shown later. Also, when plotted the intensity of loyalty over a period of time, a CLC curve can be constructed for analyzing the loyalty trend for a specific brand or company.

6 Benefit-centered Loyalty Behavior and Benefit-seeking Market Segments

Manifestation of Benefit-centered Loyalty Behavior

Obviously, the benefit-centered behavior is said to come from customer's determination to seek appropriate product-service features and benefits. Here, customers' expectation regarding product features, functions and performance are all very important and he or she may not be much concerned about the price, prompt availability or even the brand name and image of the product.

The customers of this market segment are even prepared to pay a higher price, willing to travel one extra mile, and often indifferent to brand names as long as he or she can get the right product or service. This group of customers often likes to see companies conform to quality and standards and adopting clear and explicit policies related to after-sale services. They would expect the company to deliver the promise leading to successful outcomes, both in performance and when handling complaints. Moreover, this group of customers often has high expectations as well as confidence that the company and the brand would never fail to deliver the benefits. As far as describing the customer profile of this market segment is concerned, there are four benefit seeking attributes stands out leading to four distinct micro market segments.

The Four Benefit-seeking Micro Market Segment

- Segment seeking performance assurance: This group is obsessed with product specifications, product quality, performance guarantee and promise of benefits

- Segment seeking performance: This group expects performance as promised by the provider. For them, dependability in the delivery of promise or reliability in actual performance is important. Here, promises are not always expressed explicitly by the firm but take it for granted.

- Segment seeking excellence in quality and performance: This segment is obsessed with quality and performance. He or she expects firms' commitment to excellence and delivering high degree of satisfaction

- Segment seeking convincing information about benefits: This group is very much brand conscious and therefore expects packaging and branding the above attributes with effective communication

Customer Seeking Brand Performance Assurance

Within the macro market segment of benefit-seeking customers, the first micro segment refers to the group of customers who are seeking performance assurance. By performance, it means the benefits that the product or brand is supposed to deliver to customers. It is the core or the primary and the secondary benefits and services that the brand is supposed to provide and for which the customer is expected to make a purchase. Consider, for example, the purchase of an airline ticket that guarantees a seat on a specific flight that would enable the buyer to travel from a location A to a destination B. Here, transportation from A to B on the flight on a designated seat remains the core benefit that is expected from the product. Comfort, tasty food and drinks on board, timely departure and arrival, and other related services become secondary benefits.

The primary benefit that the customer expects to enjoy is the travel between A and B and the product (or brand) performance is essentially determined by how good the customer is transported from A to B. But the other secondary benefits mentioned and augmented benefits and attributes such as convenient checking in extra baggage privilege and hospitality of the service staff etc. are all considered 'benefits and attributes' associated with the product of 'flight'.

Similarly, in the case of a tangible product, say a car that is being purchased, the core product again (primary benefit to the customer) remains transportation. The car, in addition to its brand image, is expected to have several attributes and product specifications that make this particular product or brand different from other competitor brands. The product specifications are related to the physical attributes such as shape, design and size as well as its functionality such as rate of acceleration, fuel consumption rate, speed handling and reliability on the road etc.

Moreover, there are other benefits the customer would expect. Some of these can be augmented benefits or some vital elements connected to the primary benefit. For example, reasonable refund policy of the airline management when it comes to cancellations, twenty-four hour room service in a luxury five-star hotel or after-sale and maintenance service of the automobile manufacturers are a few of such benefits the customer would have been promised and therefore expected by the customer. Prompt and effective complaint handling and resolution process is another important benefit that the companies may promise its customer. A typical customer would also expect a fair compensation in case the brand or product fails to perform as expected. Quality assurance programs and commitment to implement them effectively also give the customer's confidence on the company and their products.

An average customer of this micro segment is often well educated and rather knowledgeable about the products or services they purchase. He or she would trust the appropriate national, state, and international organizations that are normally quoted by the companies to attest or certify the specifications of their products. Certified information on the nutritional values and ingredients used in a food product, ingredients or chemical compositions of a pharmaceutical product, performance specification of a grinding machine, and ISO 9000 quality assurance are some of the examples that the customer would like to refer to before a purchase is made.

A typical customer in this segment seeks assurance about product-service quality and performance. Standards and specification of the branded product and the description of the benefits to be received are all important for this customer. This customer relies more on the written guarantees and presentation of the brand or product rather than on the promise of the service or sales staff. Moreover, this customer often tends to follow instructions as well as rules and policies.

Over a period of time, this customer begins to build trust and confidence on the company and the brand, leading to developing a sense of loyalty. The key word here is conformity that is linked to product specifications and quality assurance as well as brand performance or benefit guarantee.

Customer Seeking Brand Performance

This is the second micro segment within the 'benefit-seeking segment' and refers to the loyalty attribute of 'confidence'. It simply means delivery of promise and performance reliability. An average customer of this segment does not simply take it for granted that companies or brands would deliver what they promise. During the purchase of the flight ticket explained above, the airline company and the travel agent may give a number of specifications on benefits or attributes regarding the services. These can be the quality of food served, adequate legroom, timely departure, courtesy of the staff, connecting flights to local destinations and several other benefits. But the customer of this segment would not believe anything until he or she sees it.

Reliability and successful outcome or brand performance remains the key words for this customer. Here, she or he should be able to build up confidence that the company and its branded product and service are reliable and guaranteed to perform and the outcome is a successful event. In this regard, past experience and or references from friends and relative play an important role together with the customer's perceived image about the company and brand. A successful outcome refers to the accomplishment of all the jobs or realizing all the promised benefits, whether primary or secondary.

The profile of the average customer of this segment is characterized by having a sense of suspicion in general. He or she wouldn't take anything for granted and therefore would expect the unexpected. This customer is less panicky and less likely to vent if anything goes wrong. For this customer, it would take some time to build up confidence on new brands and companies. This sort of customer does not often trust the institutions and bureaucracy but more than likely to trust and believe word-of-mouth as well as the courteous sales staff. This customer is less likely to trust buying from the Internet or e-commerce.

For this customer, past experience, either directly or indirectly, matters most. If the past purchase experience happened to be a successful event, this customer may begin to build up confidence and trust. The average customer in this group may come from the middle class with an adequate level of education. Most likely, she or he would be of entrepreneur-type and or belonging to the achievement-driven profession such as sales and small business management. The key word here is seeing is believing and performance matters the most.

Customer Seeking Excellence in Quality

The group of customers seeking excellence in quality and satisfaction is another micro segment of the 'benefit-seeking' market segment. Typical customer of this segment expects the company to be highly committed to implementing quality assurance policies and programs. It means nothing can go wrong before, during, or even after the purchase. It is not simply the product or brand performance that this customer expects from the producer or the service provider. She or he would expect the company to perform above the norm and the product or brand performance to be excellent in providing all the promised attributes and benefits.

Imagine the customer is planning to make a room reservation at a hotel. Making a reservation itself is a pre-purchase activity where the customer may require some detailed information about the product, price, and availability on specific days etc. In the meantime, there are also some details that the reservation staff may need to know about the customer such as payment methods and credit card numbers. Here, courtesy and politeness of the hotel staff, clear description of product and benefits, cancellation policy and refund etc. all important for the customer in addition to making a confirmed reservation.

Although the 'core benefit' is a confirmed reservation by which the performance is assessed, there are other factors described constitute the secondary and augmented benefits. It is these attributes that make the entire process excellent and highly satisfactory. Not to mention the fact that if something is to go wrong in this process, it can have other costly consequences. For example, failure to allocate a specific room or not allocating rooms on the days requested can lead to greater guest dissatisfaction when the customer arrives at the hotel. The episode explained above is only one phase of the guest cycle in a hotel. When the guest is arrived, there are other core products and benefits such as providing quality accommodation as well as hoards of other secondary products such as providing food and other services. Guest's experience at the hotel is the critical phase where he or she would expect the unthinkable services with courtesy and attention from the staff.

Moreover, any dissatisfied-customer may wish to complain and therefore would expect the hotel to provide such facilities. Quality and excellence demand not only such facilities for complaint handling but also satisfactory complaint resolution process.

Profile of the typical customer of this segment may be simply described as 'difficult to satisfy' although that may not be the true in reality. This customer is either highly educated and knows about the product very well due to his or her involvement or attachment to product-service provision, or affluent and experienced due to his or her past encounters. For example, in the above hotel guest experience, the customer may be someone in the hotel profession or an affluent and experienced customer (frequent guest) who has seen the best quality product before. Imagine the expectation of a chef de cuisine when eating out in another restaurant or a system engineer when he or she wishes to buy a software program.

This customer often has the tendency to complain or just simply boycott the company or brand depending on the personality of the customer. However, a loyal repeat-customer is highly likely to complain and vent. He or she also tends to have a greater degree of loyalty once built. Also, this customer may be someone either with constructive criticism like an academic or affluent and conspicuous customer who likes to draw attention.

Customer Seeking Convincing Credible Information

This is the last micro segment of the 'benefit seeking' market segment. Typical customer of this segment expects the companies to provide appropriate, timely, convincing, and credible information on the branded product's benefits and attributes on a regular basis and when necessary. Effective communication and exchanges of views and opinion remain one of the most important factors for establishing and retaining customer relationship. Of course members of every micro segment described above require some sort of information but this segment would not act if adequate and appropriate information is not available when needed. Sometime the information can be direct and person-to-person or indirect through advertisement or some other forms of written materials. The information demanded by this group is mainly about the product benefits both core benefit and other augmented attributes.

This customer would also like to have detailed information about the companies' quality and benefit assurance policies, complaint handling and resolution policies, and customer satisfaction policies as well as testimony about the brand performance etc. In other words, it is about the other three attributes discussed in the micro-segments above. In any case, the information must be credible in the eyes of the customer of this segment.

As far as the profile of the customer in this group is concerned, it is fair to say that he or she would be an information-freak. Such a customer is also a control-freak in many ways. This customer is rather a meticulous person and would exert certain degree of resistance before committing to buy a specific brand or product. In this particular case, it would be directed towards the quality and performance of the brand and the benefit that the brand is supposed to provide.

Typical customer of this group often has the tendency to remember the brand name and attributes of the product he or she used to purchase earlier. Such customer therefore could be a loyal customer if she or he were to be convinced that the brand was guaranteed to provide the benefits and deliver performance. An average customer of this group may come from all walks of life, irrespective of the personal income or age but may seem to be a literate and educated. In an electronic market place, she or he would retrieve appropriate information from a number of sources before a commitment is made. Therefore, we can expect this customer to make informed decision.

7 Value-centered Loyalty Behavior and Value-seeking Market Segments

Manifestation of Value-centered Loyalty Behavior

Value-seeking market segment is the product of value-centered behavior. This group of people is highly conscious about product price or value of the brand. It is not simply the monetary value of the product or service that these customers are seeking but the overall value as assessed by a process of mental arithmetic. In this respect, even a promotional discount, coupons, allowances on bulk purchase as well as price stability over a period of time are all considered important by this group of customers. And, not to forget the brand image that is associated with the product price.

These customers would like to see clear and explicit company policies on pricing and expect the company to stick to their pricing policies. This market segment often monitors and evaluates competitor prices and added value of the rival products. Price stability for a reasonable period of time is therefore extremely important for these customers.

Unexpected sudden price increase would definitely harm the loyalty of these customers. If a price increase is forthcoming due to unavoidable circumstances such as the increasing cost of labor, then that needs to be effectively informed and communicated convincingly to this market segment. Moreover, perceived quality of the brand does affect the price and therefore the perceived brand value of the product. And an effective and creative communication strategy does help create this perceived value. Four value-seeking attributes and therefore four micro market segments can be identified to determine the customer profile of this market segment.

The Four Value-seeking Micro Segments

- Segment seeking assurance of the overall value of the product and price stability

- Segment seeking value and price stability in reality (while purchasing)

- Segment seeking value enhancement and satisfaction (enhanced attributes and perceived brand value)

- Segment seeking value-related information and incentives (effective communication and promotion of value attributes such as bundling and sales promotion)

Customer Seeking Value Assurance

This group of customers constitutes the first micro segment of the 'value-seeking' market segment. As in the first micro segment of the 'benefit-seeking' market segment, this group of customers seeks assurance from the companies for providing product-brand value. Value of a product is, however, difficult to be assessed easily as sometimes it is circumstantial. Nevertheless, marketers often refer value to the monetary value or the market price as perceived by the customers based on their previous experience, competitors' prices as well as the perceived quality and product benefits expected.

Whatever the definition of value may be, this customer group seeks assurance from the companies that the brand to be purchased offer value. Since most customers would refer to the price of the product when it comes to assess the value, it is important to consider the average market price of similar products that are differentiated by branding

Customers' mental arithmetic often seems good enough to calculate and assess the value of a specific brand comparatively with other brands having similar attributes that are sold in the market place. Such an assessment would also take into consideration of the extra attribute costs, such as value of time and distance that the customer may have to sacrifice, before and when a comparison is to be made.

Another important criterion of value is the stability of the monetary value or product price. This customer often remembers the price that she or he paid for the same brand last time. If additional attributes are added and a price increase in the horizon, it becomes important to inform and convince this customer in advance that he or she could still enjoys the same value. Companies often have the tendency to inflate the product price based on either profitability objectives or in line with the competitors' price. But price inflation can harm the loyalty of this group of people. This customer seeks assurance from the company that the price stability is maintained and price is managed to the mutual benefits of the customer and the company.

Concrete marketing policies regarding value assurance and price stability need to be developed if this customer is to be wooed and satisfied. Effective marketing communication campaigns, both in-house related to points of sales and external media, can be developed to inform and assure the customer about the company's commitment to offering brand value and price stability.

As far as the profile of this customer is concerned, income level of the customer should stand out. She or he should often come from middle and low-income sectors and most likely belongs to the spend-as-you-earn category. Monthly out-going of this customer often exceeds the in-take and perhaps, manages the budget with credit card or bank overdraft. Moreover, students and retirees also may fall in this category that would seek value because of their limited income. Most importantly, as an assurance seeker, this customer is conscious about his or her spending and often seems to be educated and well disciplined. Also, brand image and persuasive messages may not work miracles for this customer.

Customer Seeking Value and Price Stability

Customer of the second micro segment of this value-seeking market segment is in fact determined to attain value while purchasing and on consumption of the product. This segment enjoys and appreciates the best value that they can obtain. Most of these customers are bargain hunters and would spend time seeking out discounted brands and retailers. As in the above category, this customer is well prepared and skilled to gather information about best value brands. With the arrival of the Internet, size of this segment has grown substantially, particularly in the travel and tourism sector (such as the budget airline tickets and hotel rooms). This group of customers may also seek out opportunities of sales promotions and other discount offers. It is not surprising to see this customer walking an extra mile for a 10% discount offer or loading a full cart because of the cheap price.

When it comes to long-term loyalty for a best value product or retail store, this customer would evaluate the price stability over a period of time. For travelers seeking the best value in hotel room purchase or flight booking, Internet companies such as Lastminute.com appears to be the best choice. However, some customers in this group would consider value differently and tend to link it to product quality and enhanced attributes that they wouldn't get from an alternative product or similar brands. The latter would seek out several comparable branded products or services and evaluate the merits of value carefully before a purchase in made. In the era of e-commerce and Internet, the retail platform such as Lastminute.com versus a rival becomes the brand under evaluation rather than the products or services that are bought from such sites.

As in the above category, the profile of this group of customers can be described as bargain-seekers in general, except a minority for whom higher the value means also higher the quality and attributes. Students and retirees as well as middle and low-income groups on budget normally fall into this category. Brand image and identity may not mean anything for this customer but some do seem to appreciate the value of branded goods, especially when it becomes affordable because of discounted sales and bargain offers. In this case, this customer can become a brand-grazer, jumping from one well-recognized brand to another well-known brand.

This customer is always in the look out for bargains and promotional sales and would wait for months before a seasonal sales campaign is launched. Seasonal sales of department stores such as Marks & Spencer in the UK and Harrods in London attract thousands of customers every year. The same is true with branded discount stores such as Wall Mart. The brand image of these department stores is linked to the perception that the customers get the best value for money and therefore focusing on a segment such as this as the target market may seem an effective strategy.

Customer Seeking Value Enhancement

This group of customers not only seeks monetary value but also seems determined to get the best overall value. It means the best value for money both in terms of quality and performance as well as additional attributes and benefits that are associated with the brand. This may or may not include the monetary value such as the lowest price but the psychological attributes of value are. This micro segment of the value-seeking market segment is not bargain hunters as in the case of the above market segment in the same category instead they seek satisfaction through value enhancement, particularly through brand image.

This customer therefore seeks satisfaction from the overall value of the product purchased. In this regard, this customer is well educated and aware of the several additional attributes and benefits that the product or brand may offer on top of the core benefits expected. An average customer of this segment would expect the company to commit without any reservation to deliver value through quality and performance. He or she would trust the company reputation and the brand image to provide enhanced value and therefore would take it for granted. For this customer, quality and performance begins in the production phase such as in the quality of raw materials used in the production. Of course, enhanced attributes during the production phase to sales and after sales phases are all important if the company is to commit itself to delivering enhanced value to this customer.

Also, price stability may or may not mean anything to this customer but consistency in providing the overall value over a period of time would definitely attract the loyalty of this market segment. Although a reference price of the product may play an important role for this customer, it is the value as measured by the quality of product and services that matters the most. Product quality as per expectation does really matter for many of this customer group.

In terms of the profile of the segment, it is fair to say that this customer group consciously would evaluate the overall value of the purchase, including satisfaction that derives from psychological attributes. Contrary to the above category, this customer is rather affluent and satisfaction seeking. At times he or she may appear to be hedonistic and would be willing to pay extra for additional indulgence. Also, he or she would often evaluate the measure of enhanced value by the level of personal satisfaction, particularly during the purchase and consumption episodes.

Loyalty behavior of this customer seems to increase with higher level of satisfaction and most common examples of such behavior can be found when this customer experiences a purchase of a service product such as the hospitality services.

Customer Seeking Value-related Information

This last micro segment of the value-seeking market segment is characterized by having customers seeking information that are related to value attributes and incentive programs such as sales promotion, bulk purchase allowance, and seasonal sales etc. When it comes to the incentive programs, there are two situations here: brand-focused and brand-indifferent searches. Most Internet customers or cyber-market visitors are mainly information freaks. Some would seek information and details related product value attributes and others interested in bargains and discounts.

As seen in the above categories, most value-attributes are related to the attributes of the product or brand as well as product quality and price. Some product attributes for which the companies charge may not be essential or not so important as far as the customer expectation is concerned. This customer is keen and skilled enough to distinguish between essential product attributes and non-essential product features when it comes differentiating a brand. Therefore, information search on product value attributes is a systematic and comprehensive process, which most customers would not prefer to engage in. However, emergence of e-commerce and availability of information in the company websites as well as third party supply of easy-to-evaluate information in the Internet make this process rather interesting and entertaining for this group of customers.

In the case of incentives-seeking group, the characteristics of the customers in this market segment may appear to be rather different. For them, often the value is related to monetary price and therefore may mean bargains and promotional offers. However, it does not mean these two customer groups don't overlap. In most of the cases they do overlap and incentives and reduced price remains another value attribute. This group of customers also spends a reasonable amount of time in searching and locating bargains and other promotional incentives. Internet is again a wonderful medium for such activities. In any case, customers of this segment often know about the incentives offered in advance. Moreover, some of these customers may even belong to the sophisticated group who are very well familiar with the expensive branded goods but seeking a bargain when it comes making a purchase.

As far as the profile of this customer is concerned, it is fair to say that she or he is gifted with the availability of 'time'. This customer is patient and highly skilled in gathering and sorting information. Some of these customers would have a well-organized calendar of activities related to company sales promotions and incentive programs. This customer may come from several income levels but mainly from the middle and low-income groups. Also, a typical customer in this group is considered to be well educated and Internet savvy.

8 Convenience-centered Loyalty Behavior and Convenience-seeking Market Segments

Manifestation of Convenience-centered CLB

Customers would seek convenience in every sense when it comes to buying a product. The meaning of convenience usually cannot be defined easily. Simply put, it may mean to facilitate an event, and in this case, a purchase. By being able to purchase a product easily, one can experience convenience in most cases. It may means making the product available freely and the location of retailers or site of the service delivery facility are easily accessible. It may also mean home delivery of the product. E-marketing and e-tailing also are considered as facilitating the purchase and therefore providing convenience. In addition, convenience can also be provided by other means, such as facilitating the purchase by providing convenient payment methods.

In the end, the customers of this segment would need to be assured that the product is available conveniently and can be delivered as promised at the right place and right time. Some of the customers in this group would also like to see the company taking some efforts to satisfy the customer by being able to deliver the product in rather unusual locations and times, if necessary, irrespective of the delivery cost. Customer profile of this market segment can be determined by the four convenience-seeking attributes and therefore related micro market segments as described below.

Convenience-seeking Micro Market Segments

- Segment seeking assurance from firm for providing convenience: adequate and effective distribution system and product availability when needed as well as policy and strategy for complaints handling conveniently.

- Segment seeking product availability and convenience (adequate and accessible sales and service locations)

- Segment seeking enhanced convenience: effectiveness in supply chain management and special delivery arrangements (satisfaction) as well as venues for complaints resolutions

- Segment seeking pertinent information and effective communication about availability and other attributes of convenience (including responding to after-sales services and customer complaint)

Customer Seeking Convenience and Supply Assurance

This is the first micro segment of the 'convenience-seeking' market segment. A typical customer in this group would seek assurance from companies and producers that convenience for customers becomes an essential part of the firm's marketing policy. Here, the word convenience incorporates several attributes such as making the product or service available when needed by the customer (at the right location, time etc.) and facilitating the purchase as well as delivery of product with additional beneficial features, including after-sales services as well as convenient method for complaint handling and resolution.

This customer group expects the company to guarantee efficient and effective distribution system and convenient channels (retail outlets in accessible and nearby locations) of distribution. For some sectors, today, this may also mean availability or being able to buy via e-commerce and home delivery. A company advertising about its website so that customer can get appropriate information about the product as well as company's distribution and channel policies is a good example in this regard. Moreover, if the customer is also made known that he or she can purchase via Internet and product is delivered home next day, it would further augment the confidence factor and give assurance about providing convenience to customers.

Another example would be a hotel company promising convenience to its guests by providing adequate hotel rooms in several national and international locations. There are several examples that one can find to illustrate the policy of guaranteeing convenience by manufacturers and service companies. An automobile manufacturer often needs to guarantee the customers to provide several service locations throughout the country if customers are said to be offered convenience. So is the availability of a product, such as spare parts, whenever and wherever it is needed.

This customer thinks in advance before committing to purchase a product or brand about the convenience factor provided by the company for after-sales services. He or she is well educated and most likely to spend a good amount of time on the Internet. This customer is rather matured or seems to be over the thirties and middle age to retirees. Also, a typical customer from this segment may appear to be mobile (traveler or car owner). On the other hand, an Internet customer from this market segment may be someone working long hours and either office-ridden or home-ridden.

Customer Seeking Convenience and brand Availability

A typical customer from this micro segment is not just satisfied with promises. He or she would like to see things happening in practice. This customer is an experienced buyer and does not often trust what companies promise. Here, of course, the customer is concerned about the convenience. In other words, readily available whenever needed and wherever the product is promised to be sold. Either by experience or readily available information by the company websites or other channels, this customer knows the retail outlets or other distribution channels. Also, he or she is well informed about the fact that the product is available whenever it is searched for. Such expectations of customers come from past purchase experiences and they take it for granted that the company is very good at making this happen.

This is in fact the performance part of the convenience attribute. The company does deliver its promises and its distribution system is very effective and therefore reliable. Effective and efficient channels of distribution and reliable retail establishments on which the customer relies very much for the final outcomes for delivery are actually the factors that affect the final performance in terms of product or brand availability.

When providing this convenience factor, the logistics of warehousing and distribution also play an important role. Major transportation companies involved in the distribution of an incredible number of food items ranging from fresh to dry food cannot afford to fail if millions of customers are to be supplied with food on a daily basis, for example. What we are talking about here is the availability of an efficient and effective supply chain network and supply chain management.

Whether it is a consumer items such as food and detergents or courier mail service, this customer expects the convenience of availability and timely delivery. This customer is rather efficient and self-reliant and would expect others to be the same. There is a pretty good chance that this customer might lose his or her temper and switch brand relatively sooner if a company or brand repeatedly fail to deliver convenience as promised. An average customer of this micro segment can be a professional, entrepreneur or an economically active person working long hours. For this customer, 'what is seen is what is believed' and a positive experience is therefore said to build trust and confidence.

Customer Seeking Enhanced Convenience

This customer segment shares the same characteristics of the foregoing micro segment but, in addition, a typical customer of this segment expects more. The key word is convenience at any cost. Of course, the expectation of this customer is very high so is the satisfaction he or she seeks. There is more than one reason for such a high expectation of this customer. First, he or she may be someone who knows the convenience attributes of the product-service very well because of familiarity as a repeat customer or being a product-service provider himself or herself. Secondly, this customer may be someone who is well informed about the convenience attributes of the brand and company due to his or her curiosity and knowledge. Thirdly, this customer's cultural and demographic background, perhaps, pushes him or her to create high expectations.

The key convenience attribute is, of course, product or brand availability whenever and wherever needed by the customer. There should be a 'fail proof' marketing system that consists of an effective and successful distribution system. A typical customer in the foregoing segment would see this attributes as availability as usual at the right time and right place as well as effective and efficient channels of distribution. This may mean delivering the convenience attributes as promised. However, the customer of this micro segment would expect more than this. It would usually mean making it happen beyond expectations.

For example, suppose David is a frequent and loyal Hilton customer and he would expect a Hilton hotel room even in Timbuktu. This customer would take it for granted that the companies owe him or her something. Just imagine an American traveler in Mongolia expects replacement Travelers Checks from American Express although there wouldn't be any logistic arrangement to provide such services in that country. Often this customer is brainwashed by the brand promise.

Convenience factor in this category also includes several other attributes or benefits. For example, a company aims to facilitate credit card payment even in Saharan desert because this customer does not carry cash in hand and pays everything with credit cards in this own country. Or, just imagine this customer complaining about a brand via Internet website and expecting a reply the next minute.

The customer of this segment is sometimes well educated and has confidence on what he or she believes in. Ideally, this customer is a repeat and or seasoned customer with product-service familiarity. He or she also could be a professional involved in the provision of convenience attributes to customers with high expectations. Moreover, this customer can be someone culturally biased and would expect things as it happens in his own environment. Confidence and sometimes wealth and arrogance of some may make these customers rather unpleasant to serve at times. Loyalty of this customer is based on the promise that the firm makes and its brand reliability as perceived by the customer.

Customer Seeking Convenience-related Information

A typical customer of the last micro segment of the convenience-seeking market segment is, as in the last groups of the previous market segments, an information seeker. Appropriate and pertinent information is a must for this group of customer to act. Having time and resources to collect information often gifts this segment. Of course, here the customer is seeking information about convenience attributes. Can I easily get that when I need it? Is it available all over the country or even worldwide? Are the company and its channels of distribution effective and reliable? Is the supply chain and network managed well? If the product breaks down, can I replace it immediately? Are retails outlets available in convenient and accessible locations?

These are some of the questions this customer would ask before he or she chooses to show some attachment and loyalty to the product. So, how does this customer expect to get the right information? He or she would rely on effective communication methods that are used by the company. An Internet customer would look for company or product websites. Others would expect some form of mass communication methods such as newspaper advertisements and TV commercials. If a company wishes to attract this customer, it is essential that the communication strategy includes such information as locations, availability and complaint handling methods etc. Some of these customers would also expect the retail outlets to inform about availability through in-house communication processes.

Information about the convenience attributes is more valuable and sometimes essential for the customers of service-products such as banking, hospitality or professional services. Therefore, some of the customers of this group may be service buyers. In this day and age, most of these customers turn to the Internet where all information about the product benefits, values, as well as convenience can be found. If the brand is well-established and popular as well as available everywhere via effective and reliable network of distributors, extending the brand for another product category may also guarantee availability and convenience.

This customer may not be biased about anything first and therefore seems to be rational. He or she would first collect pertinent information and evaluate the merits of the convenience attributes before making any commitment. Since convenience is the number one priority for this customer, he or she would definitely choose the brand or product-service that would optimize the convenience factor. Quality as well as benefit attributes or price of the product may come second. This customer is a medium to long term thinker and not a hit and run person who would seek a transactional relationship with the producer or seller.

9 Image-centered Loyalty Behavior and Image-seeking Market Segments

Manifestation of Image-centered Loyalty Behavior

For some customers, image means everything. Linking the perceived brand image or company reputation to social status is rather a common phenomenon in most societies. It is fair to say that status conscious people are also image conscious customers. The status of a person is not necessarily determined by the financial or intellectual achievement or so forth. It can also be determined by one's identity, which he or she would like to attach to as in the case of youngsters to music groups and fans of sportsmen or their teams.

Brand managers have been successfully exploiting these status and identity conscious customers in order to generate brand loyalty behavior to a specific product or company brand. When a customer or group of customers act and show loyalty to a brand or company based on the perceived image, then, it is called image-centered behavior. And the customer group is called the image-seeking market segment.

Customers of this market segment live on the expectation that companies would allocate adequate resources to create a positive and popular image for the brands of products that they produce and sell. The brand image thus created and the company reputation attained are extremely important for the firm. Now the firm uses this brand image and reputation to win and retain customers. Of course, it is the product benefits, value and convenience that the customer is seeking to enjoy.

Successful outcomes are then linked to the brand name and image, which enables the company to communicate effectively with the target audience or market segment. Obviously, the customers in this group would like to see the company and brand image reinforced frequently while delivering the promise in the long run. As long as the brand image reflects the product quality, this customer will continue to follow and, convenience or price factors may not seem important. The profile of this market segment can be identified as having four micro market segments based on four image-seeking attributes as shown below.

The Four Image-seeking Micro Market Segments

- Segment seeking brand assurance or assurance of brand image and performance (powerful brand image promising to deliver benefit, value and convenience and certain other attributes such as identity, prestige and exclusivity)

- Segment seeking successful brand performance as promised (expecting to deliver brand promise, both loyalty attributes and psychological attributes such as prestige)

- Segment seeking satisfaction through enhanced brand image and company reputation (expecting to enhance and retain the brand image and reputation)

- Segment seeking the retention, protection and restoration of the company reputation and a positive brand image (creating and managing a positive brand image and company reputation as well recovering when in crisis).

Customer Seeking Brand and Reputation Assurance

This is the first micro segment of the image-seeking market segment. A typical customer of this group seeks assurance on providing a powerful brand image as well as brand performance. This customer needs assurance that the company and the brand will have a special place in the society or sub-culture, in which the customer desires to be a member. This may even linked to a sub-culture such as the fans of a famous football team. Here, the customer is seeking assurance that the brand would provide some identity, belongingness or prestige. For example, if this customer is assured that the product brand is sold only in the exclusive department stores, then that would provide some psychological benefits. The brand image that this customer expects is usually identity, prestige, perceived quality, and exclusivity etc.

The second assurance that this customer seeks is on the brand performance. In this regards, it may mean the promised benefit attributes as well as other attributes such as value and convenience. Here, the company needs to convince the customer that the brand name stands for quality and value as well as an impeccable performance record. The loyalty attributes discussed before are tied together here and packaged and bundled to the brand name and the image that it carries.

The art and tools of communication and the effectiveness of the campaign used play an important role in convincing this customer about the brand assurance for image and performance. The use of modern technology in the preparation of TV commercial has made this job much easier today. However, creating an image assurance that is linked to psychological factors is not an easy task. Brand extension strategy (extending a proven and successful brand to include other products) used by companies and the company reputation in the past etc., can also assure the customer that the new brand under consideration can deliver the attributes that this customer desires or expects.

The profile of this customer is not only characterized by having those attributes such as the desire to seek identity and prestige as well as performance but also need to be assured that the brand (and company) is capable of delivering them. An average customer may be educated but he or she can come from any background and age groups. However, rather sophisticated communication methods that need to be employed to deliver the assurance message require this customer to be well-educated and often experienced with familiarity of techniques and media used. However, the cultural factor of the customer may mean difference in how the message is structured and communicated.

Customer Seeking Brand Performance

This group of the image-seeking market segment would like to see brand performance in reality and assurance is not just enough. By performance, it means the delivery of all those benefits and attributes that the brand had promised to deliver. Of course, the customer expectation in this group is high and the brand name is positively fixed in their mind. Performance also means delivering the psychological benefits that the customer expects from the purchase of a specific brand of product. This is what we mean by such attributes as prestige or identity etc.

In the highly competitive world of branded goods and services, customers are often seen confused where sustaining brand loyalty is extremely difficult. For many, affinity to a specific brand is a process of gradual build up after numerous trials and testing.

This is what the author calls 'Brand Ratification' - approval and acceptance of a brand. But for some, an attachment to a brand name may come by much faster or even unexpectedly because of the nature and type of affiliation and links the brand is associated with. For example, when a well known and award winning sportsman is seen wearing a PUMA t-shirt, his fans would create an affinity to the same brand, perhaps, unconsciously. Recent outburst of sports-related sponsorships has seen as remarkably effective for the companies trying to create brand awareness and affinity. However, the cost of such sponsorships and other marketing promotion campaigns requires the customer to bear the burden of cost. With this comes also the profit.

Nevertheless, there is a problem of brand performance in general. If the brand does not provide the expected benefits, customer would be extremely disappointed. Who wouldn't be disappointed if the $200 PUMA shoes did not live up to the expectation when almost similar non-branded (or cheaper brands) shoes could be bought for just $25. After all, there are numerous copies or duplicates available in the market today that makes the problem even worst. However, customers of this micro segment of the market are often seemed to be careful and would be prepared to pay the demanding price for the original product. They may even show some degree of obsession to the brand but with high expectations.

When the brand fails to deliver as expected, the loyal customer would still have hope but repeat failures would soon force the customer to rethink about brand loyalty. This customer may come from all walks of life but often educated and middle to high-income group. Like in the same categories of benefit or value seeking segments, this group of customers can be satisfied with the brand's performance in delivering the actual product (benefits) performance. No matter how much obsessed this customer may become, there is always a possibility that he or she may leave the brand if it does not deliver the expected benefits. However, this customer may not be willing to pay an outrageous price just for the sake of brand name either.

Customer Seeking Enhanced Brand Satisfaction

This group of customers seeks high degree of satisfaction from the overall performance of a branded product and its brand image itself. The brand image of the product and the company reputation are highly sought after by this group of customers. In addition to the brand performance in terms of delivering the product benefits as promised, this customer often seeks more, particularly the psychological benefits of affiliating the buyer to the perceived image of the brand and corporate reputation. The prestige of the brand, the identity that brings to the buyer or user, and the image and reputation of the company or organization that produces and sells are all important psychologically to this customer group.

The customers of this micro-segment are rather difficult to be satisfied merely by the brand performance. Some degree of fanatics and high level of obsession often characterize the brand affinity of these customers. Even if the brand fails to perform materially, the loyal customers won't be put off easily as long as the dream is kept alive which normally most brand mangers tend to do. The obsessed customer would still hang on to it until truth is discovered. But repeated failure to honor the promises would take this customer by surprise and leave no other choice other than to exit.

This customer is typically an emotionally inclined person with a tendency to manifest high degree of obsession (to person or things). The profile of this customer group is almost same as the above group except the later is highly obsessed and even fanatics. They may come from all walks of life, from poor to rich and young to old.

The less wealthy would save money to buy a specific brand of product that is often expensive. Unlike in the above group, it is the intangible attributes that these customers are craving for. And the high degree of satisfaction that these customers seek is from those intangible or psychological benefits. This is what most of the brand managers and advertisers often try to focus when it comes to measuring the brand performance.

Seeking Brand Reputation (protection and restoration)

This is a special group of customers within the image-seeking market segment who already have the confidence on the positive image of the brand and or corporation. This group emerges from the previous groups of customers in the same market segment but would like to carry on with the existing image. These customers would like to see the companies take necessary and timely actions to protect the existing brand image or even corporate reputation. The protection would guarantee them the retention or maintenance of the existing image. In other words, this group of customers expects the companies to keep up to their brand promise by continuing to deliver the required brand performance. It is a long-term commitment. The image retention strategy may also require to considering image enhancement techniques too.

In case the brand or company breaks the promise either accidentally or by an unexpected event, remedial action is warranted immediately. Restoration of the image held or rebuilding a positive brand image and corporate reputation as expected remain number one priority. Honest and transparent communication and an effective marketing communication campaign such as public relation efforts may be needed in order to restore the lost image or recover from a crisis. What is particularly important is to communicate with the existing target market and especially with this group of customer.

The profile of this group of customers is almost the same as the previous group of customers but they are also well-seasoned loyal customers. Their confidence is very difficult to be shaken by a trivial mistake or unexpected crisis in brand performance. These customers would go for searching facts and detailed information in order to prove and rationalize that their confidence in the brand is not at vein. It is very important and cannot-afford-to-lose sort of customers. The recent problem of TOYOTA with sudden acceleration and failing brake system may make millions of customers wonder if quality is at stake. But, the faithful would still find it difficult to abandon their favorite brand. It is extremely important that the company recognizes these customers and communicates with them effectively and on a timely basis. The emphasis is on continued brand performance and communication.

10 Managing Customer Brand Loyalty
(Brand Loyalty and Customer Retention Strategy)

A Framework for Managing Customer Brand Loyalty

Our key objective here is to develop a framework to manage customer brand loyalty strategically over a period of time. This may require long term parameters such as what sort of market segments the company should be targeting in the long run. Since the market segments identified in this book are derived from loyalty-led behavior, identifying and managing a few appropriate market segments would enable the company to achieve its goal of managing customer brand loyalty effectively.

In the previous chapter, a framework has been established to segment the market using the CLB determinants. As a result, we have identified four major areas of loyalty behavior determinants: benefit-centered, value-centered, convenience-centered, and image-centered behavior segments. By further classification of these behavior segments based on the loyalty criteria of conformity, confidence, commitment, and communication, we were able to identify sixteen market segments that were derived from customer loyalty behavior as described in the previous chapter.

The Customer Loyalty Management (CLM) Strategy, as in any other strategy framework, requires us to first carry out an analysis of the current situation. It means the understanding of the current level of customer loyalty towards the company and its products or brands that are currently offered. If the company offers more than one brand or product, it may be necessary to examine them independently.

However, loyalty to a brand or company cannot be assessed in isolation. Customers' loyalty towards the company that manufactures the product and the intermediary firms through which it reaches the ultimate consumer are also should be taken into consideration. The strategy framework shown here (figure 1) should help us understand the entire process involved in the strategic management of customer brand loyalty.

Brand strategy is only one aspect of the overall marketing strategy. For a retail firm, the corporate brand name remains the focus. But, for other firms, whether with a single product or multi products, the focus may be on the product brand or brands. The framework provided here enables the marketer to assess and develop a management strategy for each brand independently although it needs to be derived from the firm's overall marketing strategy.

Corporate Marketing Strategy

The corporate marketing strategy is the marketing master plan that describes the firm's long-term marketing goals and objectives as well as the ways to achieve those desired states in the future. If yours is not a large corporation but a small company with one or two branded products, you may call it simply a marketing strategy. The key characteristics of this plan are visionary and proactive with long-term and flexible objectives as well as having alternative proposals or strategies to achieve them.

Obviously, the master plan would also consist of a blueprint for implementing the plan. Consequently, the plan for implementation is said to have several strategic marketing programs with specific action plans. The plan is not complete without an evaluation strategy to monitor and assess the implementation process as well as the overall success of the master plan in achieving the corporate marketing goals and objectives.

Marketing goals and objectives are always linked to describing certain desired outcomes that are often related to company products and its market. Goals are often vague and points out the direction of the desired states. Objectives are derived from the goals but with specific targets or dimensions such as time frame and quantities for achievement. Therefore, any marketing objectives that the company sets should be either measurable or verifiable so that they can be evaluated for effectiveness or success.

Corporate marketing goals often would emphasize the desired directions such as successful new product development, market leadership, competitive advantage over rivals, product and market diversification, product differentiation, and market penetration and growth etc. Marketing objectives, in the meantime, identify specific areas within each direction with clear targets and dimensions that are achievable. For example, in the area of new product development, the objective may be to improve the features and attributes of an existing product to beat the rivals or to introduce a new product to replace an existing product that is in the declining stage of the product life cycle (PLC). Here, the objective would clearly identify the type of improvement (in attributes) or the nature and type of a new product to be developed. Also, it would specify the required time frame for development and the estimated time of test market and product launch.

Most important of all corporate goals are growth and profitability. These two goals are again linked to the above marketing goals and objectives identified. Growth and profitability cannot be achieved without a strong and growing customer base. Then the next questions are how can a firm enjoy the loyalty of its customer who would continue to buy the product or brand? How can a firm find new customers who would become loyal and join the already existing customers in order to support the firm's growth?

Figure 1: CLM Strategy Framework

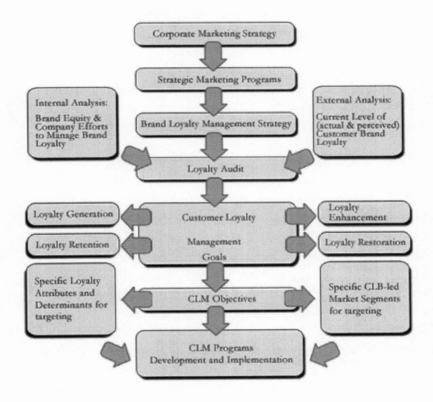

As we have seen before, here loyalty is of course a commodity or product for sale. And the seller is the customer while the buyer is the firm. This exchange process, which is the reverse of the traditional method, is more than the fundamental exchange of goods and money. In addition, the firm has to offer more than just the product or brand in order to buy the customers' loyalty.

In order to achieve growth and profitability, the company therefore may have to identify the appropriate strategic marketing goals such as market leadership and diversification. Achieving these goals constitutes the development and implementation of specific strategic marketing programs such as the CLM strategy.

Strategic Marketing Programs: CLM Strategy

Strategic Marketing Programs such as the CLM are long-term in nature but action-driven. Other such commonly implemented programs include Customer Relationship Management and Integrated Marketing Communication etc. Companies do have several loyalty programs such as the frequent-flier programs in airlines and frequent-guest membership programs in hotels and casinos. But these have never been considered as strategic marketing programs. Moreover, the concept of loyalty or its definition and understanding were rather limited and vague as used in these programs.

The proposed program of CLM is however strategic in nature and scope. It's a long-term strategy that requires insights and flexibility. Since customer loyalty has been defined as the attitude and behavior resulting in tangible actions of purchasing specific goods and services, its continuity is said to depend on several factors. Also, the major axiom of BLM is that the brand loyalty curve over a period of time passes through three key stages of growth, maturity and decline as in the product life cycle (PLC).

Loyalty as a Product and Managing Brand Loyalty

The core of the customer brand loyalty management (BLM) strategy rests with the development of the 'loyalty product' itself. Since customer brand loyalty is a product as defined in chapter two, understanding the nature and characteristics as well as the components of the loyalty product is extremely important. As in the product life cycle, customer brand loyalty is also said to pass through the stages of growth, maturity, and decline in the absence of any deliberate actions taken by the company to regularly restore the brand loyalty curve. We call the brand loyalty curve as the Brand Loyalty Life Cycle (LLC) or you may want to call it the product life cycle of brand loyalty.

Developing a loyalty product strategy requires us to identify and determine specific product goals and objectives. These would remain the goals and objectives of the CLM strategy itself. In doing so, first, we need to assess the current level of customer brand loyalty as perceived by the target market groups of the brand or company in question. This would represent as the external analysis. Similarly, for an internal analysis, it is required to assess the brand's capability (including brand equity) and also the company's effort to manage the product called customer brand loyalty. These analyses would lead us to setting appropriate CLM goals and objectives.

This in turn would require us to carry out a brand loyalty audit that consists of both the internal (brand attributes and efforts to manage brand loyalty) and external factors (actual brand loyalty and loyalty as perceived by the target customers). Obviously, such an audit would reveal the strength and weakness of the factors that determine the brand loyalty environment as well as the emerging opportunities and threats externally.

11 Customer Loyalty Audit: External Analysis

Level of Brand Loyalty as Perceived by Customers

External analysis refers to the assessment of the overall customers' perception on the level of loyalty that they have on a specific brand or company. The object of analysis is the brand or company and the subject is the intensity of loyalty that a specific group of customers or market segment shows towards the brand. Therefore, it is an analysis of group loyalty rather than individual brand loyalty. For this reason, it is important to examine the CLB-led market segmentation model discussed in the previous chapter. Once the appropriate market segments are identified as the target markets of a specific brand, it would be easier to consider an effective methodology for measuring the intensity of customer brand loyalty. The assessment refers to the aggregate intensity of brand loyalty as perceived by a specific group of customers.

A Framework for Loyalty Assessment

There can be numerous reasons why someone should remain loyal to a brand or company since there are several factors seem to influence customer brand loyalty. It also means measuring brand loyalty objectively is rather a difficult task. Perhaps, it is much easier to understand why someone would exit or switch a brand or company than to know why he or she should remain attached to it. For example, it is not really difficult to understand why a customer switches brand when the product fails to function as expected or unable to provide the attributes and benefits that the customer is seeking. Similarly, it is clear that a customer would definitely seek an alternative brand when the price of the product becomes unaffordable. What about customer seeking alternatives or switching brand when the favorite brand becomes inaccessible or difficult to find in convenient locations such as in retail outlets? In fact, this may appear to be a strong case of motivation to try a different brand or company although the quality and price of the current brand may be acceptable and affordable respectively. However, a customer seeking alternative brands because of deficiency in brand image or company reputation may seem a little difficult to understand at first.

If one finds it difficult to link the brand image of specific product to its benefits or other good attributes, then he or she may not be induced to establish or continue to have an affinity. Here, only an effective and creative marketing communication campaign can establish this link. Similarly, when the brand image is unexpectedly ruined due to a crisis, resurrection is extremely difficult. Even powerful public relation campaigns and media management may not be helpful in bringing back the trust. In that case, a thorough well planned Bounce Back Strategy (BBS) may be needed.

If the causes of loyalty behavior and continued attachment of customer to a brand can be explained by the four factors of *continuity variable* and each can be determined by the four strategic Cs as seen in the CLB-led market segmentation, then we may be able to establish some instruments to measure the intensity of customer loyalty objectively. According to the segmentation grid described in the previous chapter, there are 16 loyalty behavior segments (four key segments with four sub-segments in each) that can be used to identify appropriate instruments for measuring the perceived level of customer brand loyalty.

There may be more than one appropriate instrument for every sub-segment. The author here has identified two instruments for each of the 16 market segments based on the characteristics of each segments. Please refer to appendix A for these characteristics.

CLB-led Segmentation and Loyalty Assessment

The characteristics of the CLB-centered market segments remain useful and can be used to develop instruments to measure the level of intensity of brand loyalty. Here, the sixteen different micro segments under the four key market segments based on the attributes of Benefit-centered, Value-centered, Convenience-centered, and Image-centered behaviors are examined before developing instruments for measuring the intensity of brand loyalty. It should however be noted that more than two instruments can be developed for every segment, if necessary although the author considers only two instruments here.

Measuring Customer Brand Loyalty

The measurement of intensity of brand loyalty demands an important question regarding its real purpose. The ultimate objective of the entire process is to assess the current level of customer loyalty at any given time for a specific brand so that appropriate CLM goals and objectives can be set. Nevertheless, the instruments provided as an example (in appendix A) reflects the generic nature of measurement. It means we can use the survey instruments provided to determine the loyalty behavior of any group of customers for any brands. In other words, to identify what attributes and determinants of loyalty can help generate brand loyalty as perceived by the customers.

For example, take the case of loyalty determinant C2 or 'confidence' and the loyalty attribute 'brand benefit' (Diagram 1: Sub-segment C2-B: Confidence-Benefit) from the survey questionnaire as shown below. Here, the units of measurement are shown under the 'characteristics column' and the measuring instruments are under the 'instrument column'. The instruments are survey instruments to be used for assessing the level loyalty that the customer is prepared to show based on the characteristics in the left column.

Diagram 1: Sub-segment C2-B

Characteristics	Instruments
Reliability in delivering brand attributes and benefits.	I would continue to buy a brand if I am convinced that it would deliver benefits as promised according to specifications.
Successful brand outcome & satisfactory performance.	I would continue to buy a brand if it performs satisfactorily by delivering the benefits as expected.

The loyalty determinants of this sub-segment are obviously two parts: how confident the customers are that a brand is 1) reliable to deliver benefits according to specifications and 2) guaranteed to perform satisfactorily (successful outcome). If these two conditions are met, the assumption is that the customers would continue to buy the brand and therefore expected to continue to show some form of loyalty towards a brand. In this case, the customer could be any potential buyer and the product could be anything in the market irrespective of their specific brand names.

In other words, these are generic instruments that can be used irrespective of the target groups or brands. A survey research such as this can be carried out to assess the importance of loyalty attribute factors and loyalty determinants as seen by the different customer groups for any brand. Obviously, what constitutes or generate brand loyalty can vary from culture to culture; country to country; society to society; and one social group to another group as defined by demographic or psychographic factors.

How much emphasis a customer places and how he or she perceives the contents and importance of these determinants would reveal the role of the above instruments in assessing the customer brand loyalty in general. Of course, depending on the age and other demographic factors of the respondents, the average ratings of a group of customers can vary to some extent. Nevertheless, if customers were asked to rate these instruments on an eleven-point scale of 0 to 10 using such statements as non-agreeing to fully agreeing (survey instruments as shown in the box), a rating of 5 would indicate a neutral score. In the meantime, an average score of 8 for both of the statements would reveal that the respondent agrees with the behavioral attributes implied.

In order to examine this in detail, the author undertook a pilot study in 2005 using a suburban university town of BILKENT (where the author was a teaching staff at the university) in Ankara, Turkey. The study consisted of two stages (or two case studies as seen appendix B and C); first one was about brand loyalty in general to the product category of instant coffee and the seconds study was related to a specific brand of instant coffee.

From the first study, it was possible to assess the role of both loyalty attributes and loyalty determinants in generating brand loyalty as well as the differences between them as perceived by the different (age groups) segments of the participants groups. As far as the attributes were concerned, all four variables (benefit, value, convenience, and image) seemed to have contributed equally to generating brand loyalty but benefit and convenience variables stood out as significant. In the case of loyalty determinants (conformity, confidence, commitment, and communication), the second variable confidence and the third variable commitment were perceived as significant by the participants (see case study 1 in appendix B).

The second study (case study 2 in appendix C) conducted after a month using a selected group of participants from the previous study was aimed at assessing their brand loyalty to a specific brand of instant coffee. Here, the survey instruments were slightly modified to reflect the specific brand studied. From the first case study, it was possible to assess (scores) the main causes of loyalty among the four loyalty attributes and four determinants. In the meantime, it was also possible to see how these triggers have been distributed among the loyalty attributes and determinants (tables A and B in appendix B). This in fact helped to assign weights as shown in table D in appendix B. Table 1 below shows the total scores obtained for the specific brand of instant coffee from study 2 (scores of loyalty attributes corresponding to loyalty determinants as shown in table C in appendix B).

Table 1: Loyalty Scores for Brand 'A' Instant Coffee

Loyalty Determinants	Loyalty Attributes				
	Benefit	Value	Convenience	Image	Total
Conformity	12	10	12	14	48
Confidence	15	12	15	15	57
Commitment	13	10	14	10	47
Communication	14	12	12	16	54
Total Score	54	44	53	55	206

As far as the loyalty determinants (conformity, confidence, commitment, and communication) are concerned, it becomes clear from the above table that confidence factor or brand performance in reality (highest score) and communication factor or promotion remained important with high scores (vertical total score column). But, when it came to examining the loyalty attributes (benefit, value, convenience, and image), the total scores for all variables remained high except the value attribute. Tables 2 and 3 below show the total loyalty determinant scores and total loyalty attributes scores together with the final loyalty indices calculated using the weighted average scores (please refer to tables C and D in appendix B for further details).

Table 2: Loyalty index according to Loyalty Determinants

	Conformity	Confidence	Commitment	Communication
Total Scores	48	57	47	54
Weighted Aver. Index	60.00	71.25	58.75	67.5

Table 3: Loyalty Index According to Loyalty Attributes

	Benefit	Value	Convenience	Image
Total Scores	54	44	53	55
Weighted Aver. Index	67.50	55.00	66.25	68.75

The assessment of the current level of customer loyalty is an external analysis and akin to the assessment of opportunity and threat in the SWOT analysis. Considering customer loyalty as a product in its own right, we can also determine its product life cycle or what we call the Brand Loyalty Life Cycle (BLLC).

In order to construct a BLLC, loyalty indices, preferably the attribute loyalty BVCI loyalty indices are needed to be obtained for over a period of time for the same brand using the same market segment observed. The aggregate loyalty indices taken every year, say for a period of 4 or 5 years can be plotted along the Y-axis (dependent variable) using time in years as values for X-axis (independent variable). Since the trend would indicate whether the loyalty is growing or stabilized or even declining, we should be able to determine the appropriate stage of customer brand loyalty in its BLLC curve.

Plotting the BLLC Curve

Suppose we want to plot the brand loyalty life-cycle curve for brand 'A' instant coffee that we discussed before using the aggregate attribute-led (BVCI Loyalty) loyalty index as shown below.

Table 4:

Attribute-led Loyalty Indices for Brand 'A' Instant Coffee

Loyalty Attributes	Year 1	Year 2	Year 3	Year 4	Year 5
Benefit	14.58	15.00	15.20	14.90	14.80
	67.50%	69.62%	70.27%	68.98%	68.68%
Value	10.12	10.00	10.10	09.60	09.36
	55.00%	54.54%	54.89%	51.17%	51.00%
Convenience	14.31	14.52	14.57	14.52	14.52
	66.25%	67.22%	67.45%	67.22%	67.30%
Image	12.65	13.20	13.22	13.26	13.28
	68.75%	71.74%	71.80%	72.06%	72.17%
Aggregate Index	51.66	52.76	53.08	52.28	52.00
	64.57%	65.95%	66.35%	65.35%	65.00%

If we assume that we have the loyalty indices for brand 'A' for the last 5 or 6 years from the annual survey research conducted in BILKENT as shown above, then we can proceed to plotting the BLLC curve for the said brand. The numbers are hypothetical.

Please note that in order to get the percentage indices for benefit and convenience attributes, we need to divide their figures by 21.6 and for the value and image attributes, their figures need to be divided by 18.4. This is because, the weighting for the former two attributes was 0.27 (27%) and the latter two it was 0.23 (23%). The potential total for each is 80 where the sum of weights should be 100% (please see appendix B for detail). In order to plot the brand loyalty life cycle from the data shown in the above table, we need to use the year as the horizontal axis (or X-axis) and the aggregate loyalty index as vertical or Y-axis as shown below:

Diagram 2: BLLC Curve for Brand 'A' Instant Coffee

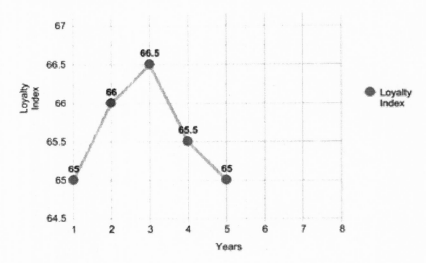

It is interesting to note here that the aggregate loyalty curve is slipping down after peaking up during the third year. However, careful observation would tell that the downward slope is due to slipping attributes of 'value' and to some extent 'benefit' (refer to the above table). In the same time, customers did not seem to have concerns about the 'convenience' attribute of product availability. Obviously, image-led loyalty behavior has enhanced during the period of five years. Although it illustrates a hypothetical case, it does not seem to be far from reality. When companies, try to create a powerful brand image, other factors such as brand benefits become a secondary issue. Negligence and complacence factors do play a role here. Heavily promoted and branded product often tends to sell for high prices until the customer perception on the value reaches low level. Also, when the demand for a branded product increases, even the lack of availability becomes a problem sometimes.

It is also useful to note that we can plot independent loyalty attribute curves for every BVCI attributes along with the aggregate attribute-led loyalty life-cycle curve. The above table has relevant figures, for example, for all the four BVCI attributes and should remain helpful even if we don't intend to draw the loyalty life-cycle curves separately.

Interpretation of the Brand Loyalty Life Cycle

As we have noted earlier, the loyalty life cycle curve for a specific brand can have three distinct stages when examined over a long period of time. It is often difficult to pin point the entry stage of the life cycle for a popular brand in the market. However, when a well-known brand is introduced newly to a foreign market, for example, its chronology can be recorded and the brand history can be traced. Here, the ideal time to monitor and track the brand loyalty behavior would be from the beginning of the second year. It does not mean that the brand loyalty curve cannot be tracked anytime as we did for the instant coffee above.

Based on the resources made available and the effort that the brand manager and the marketing department usually make to launch a new brand in the market, the initial stage of the loyalty curve tends to slope up. The brand awareness campaign and sales promotion campaigns at the beginning, although expensive, do provide an opportunity for the customer to flirt with brand loyalty. If customer expectations are met as well as the brand delivers as promised, the flirting customer would gradually build up confidence and an affinity towards the brand would increase. Repeat purchase would reinforce the confidence leading to building a bond. But, in order to facilitate a repeat purchase, the brand manger and the company may have to do a lot more.

The four loyalty attributes of benefit, value, convenience, and image speak up a lot here. Some would expect the product to be exceptionally good in satisfying customer by delivering the product benefits in order to bring them closer. Another group would expect the product or brand to be of exceptional value, often measured in monetary terms. It may be the availability factor that would necessitate the repeat purchase for another group. And for some others, it may be the convincing communication and brand image as perceived by them that would encourage the repeat purchase.

The customer would often evaluate the new brand carefully in comparison with his or her existing brand or brands in delivering the four attributes. Eventually, if the new brand is perceived as better than the existing brand, repeat purchase begins and consistent brand performance thereafter would lead to starting a love affair. This is what we call the maturity stage of the loyalty life cycle.

During the maturity stage, the customer is prepared to give the benefit of the doubt even when the brand fails to satisfy occasionally. Most companies and brand managers try to sustain the customer brand loyalty through effective communication and creating a powerful brand image rather than providing other attributes. In most cases at this stage, the quality of the product may begin to slip as the company becomes complacent. Moreover, the product price usually peaks up, especially when the company tries to skim profit during the best time. Although the channels of distribution can be effective and product availability is almost assured, soaring demand may cause problem with supply chain management. All these three factors when act together may have a cumulative negative effect on the brand loyalty curve that would pull the life cycle downwards. This stage is called decline or disloyalty stage. If this situation continues with further frustration and dissatisfaction, customer would seek to exit whenever an opportunity arises (for a detailed discussion on BLLC, please see chapter 2).

Current Level of Brand Loyalty

At this point, what seems important is to assess the level of brand loyalty of a specific market segment as we have done above. In addition to the above analysis of the attribute-led brand loyalty behavior, we can also assess the attitudinal loyalty using the four determinants of loyalty attributes (4Cs: conformity, confidence, commitment, and communication). The customer perception on the importance of these determinants in generating loyalty attributes can be measured as in table A (in appendix B) horizontally and the aggregate loyalty index for each of the determinant can be obtained as shown in table C (appendix B). Even these loyalty indices can change over a period of time for a specific market segment.

Therefore, here we have a number of key assessment criteria: the individual loyalty index of the four attributes of BVCI and the overall behavioral loyalty index; the attitudinal loyalty index of the individual determinants of four Cs; and the stage of the loyalty indices in the BLLC curve.

If a nationwide loyalty index is required, the survey research can be duplicated using several representative samples taken from specific cities or towns before an aggregate index is obtained. Only a professional market research organizations or experienced researcher should be involved in conducting the survey.

The key objective of the assessment exercise is to determine if the current level of brand loyalty as perceived by the customers and to assess whether there emerges any specific trend or pattern such as declining or increasing etc. Also, from the analysis shown above, it is possible to pinpoint the specific factor or attributes that causes the emerging pattern. Based on the overall position of the loyalty index in the BLLC, it is also possible to interpret the characteristics of the situation. All of these results then should be matched with the level of effort the company and the managers have taken to generate and enhance brand loyalty so that appropriate goals and objectives for the brand management strategy can be set.

One should not however confuse the BLLC with that of product or brand life cycle. It should be noted that a product (or brand) life cycle is plotted using only the total annual revenue or the volume in output sold annually over a period of time. It is always possible for the product or brand life cycle to grow or remain stable while the brand loyalty curve continues to decline or vice versa. This is because customers can continue to buy a brand even though their loyalty to the brand may be slipping. Similarly, customers with a strong loyalty behavior may find it difficult to buy the brand for various reasons. Nevertheless, at times, it may be possible to see the BLLC and PLC to exhibit some degree of similarity.

12 Brand Loyalty Audit: Internal Analysis

Brand Loyalty Strength as Perceived by the Firm

Having examined the level of brand loyalty as perceived by the customers in the external analysis, it is important that we now proceed to assess the brand strength in terms of loyalty as well as the effectiveness of the strategies and efforts that the company has undertaken to generate and manage brand loyalty within. Although most firms do not have any explicit goals or objectives to generate or manage customer brand loyalty, some believe that it is the creation of a powerful brand name and image that does this function.

In this respect, most companies spend millions of dollars and employ the best in the sector to help develop successful brand names and to manage the brand image even if they have one already. For many, unfortunately, brand loyalty remains a misunderstood concept. Nevertheless, brand name and image do play a part in the process of generating and boosting customer brand loyalty.

The common brand assessment that most firms care about is the concept called brand equity. This can be considered as the power and value that the brand has over the consumers' mind. In other words, it is the extent to which the customers are willing to pay more for the brand because of the image and the confidence that they have on the brand. This also leads us to define brand equity as the brand value. However, putting a number to brand value or equity is difficult but subjective measurement and industry estimates remain the common practice.

As far as our internal assessment is concerned, it can be attributed to the tangible result and verifiable actions that the company has carried out in order to generate and boost the brand loyalty. Also, the collective perception of the managers based on external surveys as well as internal records of sales and revenue can further add weights to the assessment outcomes. Nevertheless, it is extremely important that the assessment exercise is carried out for each and every brand independently.

Assessment Method

The method outlined here for the internal assessment incorporates the same criteria that we used for external analysis. The customer brand loyalty attributes of benefit, value, convenience, and image and the first four determinant variables of loyalty, conformity, confidence, commitment and communication are again used here to develop an assessment framework. The entire process consists of two stages: one is the brand performance audit based on the perception of the brand managers and brand executives, including the sales staff; and the other is the brand expenditure and outcome audit based mainly on the account of the strategic cost centers that are related to managing the brand.

The Brand Performance Audit

This audit is a simple survey of the executives and staff involved in managing the brand. The participants should be chosen based on their knowledge of the said brand through their involvement in product development, production, customer service, sales, costing & pricing, promotion, and distribution. Some of the top managers, including the brand managers and marketing executives will also be part of the survey. However, the sample size would not support the view that survey results can be scientifically validated. We can use either the Delphi technique of expert opinion survey where the participants' opinion is modified based on the consensus, or Decision Calculus method where the judgments are weighted and validated using statistical methods based on the number of judges. Here again, the criteria used to rate the expert opinion are the same as in the external analysis. On a scale of 0 to 10, the participants will rate the brand's performance based on the attributes of 'benefit', 'value', 'convenience', and 'image'.

As we have noted before, the benefit attribute refers to the product feature and characteristics such as quality as well as the benefits that the customers are seeking from the product. Value attribute of the brand refers to the monetary value or price as well as price stability over a period of time. The attribute of convenience is mainly the availability of the brand conveniently when needed by the customers and efficiency and effectiveness of the channels of distribution. The last attribute of image refers to the brand perception and image that are ingrained in the customers' mind. It also refers to the effectiveness of the promotion campaigns and marketing communication strategies in general. As far as the best method is concerned, the Delphi Technique seems favorable. Since not all participants are knowledgeable about all the four variables of attributes, consensus method of expert opinion survey method is therefore recommended. When rating the brand performance based on their opinion, participants should consider the four conditions or criteria identified before: conformity, confidence, commitment, and communication.

Case Study

This case study refers to the product of 'instant coffee' that we have already examined in the external analysis. The brand name is: 'A' and the brand performance audit is based on the expert opinion survey of 15 respondents (or brand representatives, members of the sales & marketing and production team) involved with this brand. However, unlike in the previous case studies, this is a hypothetical study.

Table 5: Brand Performance Audit

Loyalty Attributes

Loyalty Determinants	Benefit	Value	Conve-nience	Image	Total Score
Conformity	13	12	14	16	55
Confidence	14	14	15	18	62
Commitment	16	10	14	16	58
Communication	14	11	12	16	52
Total Score	57	47	55	68	227

The above table is the same as table 1 in external assessment (previous chapter) and the method of assessment and instruments used are almost the same. However, the score of the four C determinants are assessed from two survey instruments but combined to produce a single score as seen in the above table. It is important that the respondents in this survey should be made aware of the overall historic and the current levels of performance of the brand under consideration.

Nevertheless, there are a few differences between the customer survey in the external assessment and brand performance audit in the internal analysis. The sample size of the former was large and could be statistically validated. The respondents in the latter were intended to be only a handful of people linked to the brand within the company and considered as having expert knowledge about at least some aspects of the brand. The resulting rates were not weighted in the case of the latter but converged based on the consensus of the participants. The sum of the score of 227 is 71% of the total of 320. Simply put, the Brand Performance Index is seen as 0.71 or 71%. This score when compared with the customer brand loyalty index of 64.57% in case study 1, it may seem much better than expected. It could also mean that the management expectation (brand management staff) of customer brand loyalty does not match the actual level of brand loyalty as seen by the customers. One good reason for this would be evident from the scores of 'image attributes' as rated by the in-company team. There is always a tendency for the company to spend money on expensive image building PR campaigns that are perceived by the management as tools to boost brand loyalty.

Brand Expenditure and Outcome Audit

The brand expenditure and outcome audit is simply an analysis of the total item costs and the outcomes as relevant to boosting or maintaining the brand loyalty level. The cost centers or cost items are again listed by four major loyalty attributes: benefit, value, convenience, and image. Similarly, the outcomes of the key expenditure items are also identified and listed under the loyalty attributes (see below).

Table 6: Brand Expenditure Audit

Cost of providing Benefit Attributes	Cost of providing Value Attributes	Cost of providing Convenience Attributes	Cost of providing Image Attributes
Product improvement	*Total value of discount offered*	*Production stability*	*Brand image improvement*
Quality assurance and control	*Special offers & promotions*	*Cost of channel improvements*	*Image (PR/AD) maintenance*
Complaint resolution	*Cost of price stability – opportunity cost*	*Logistic improvement*	*Image recovery (PR/AD)*
CRM/Customer service		*Cost of special delivery*	*Sponsorships & promotions*
		Supply chain management	*Corporate reputation*
Total cost as a percentage of Revenue	Total cost as a percentage of Revenue	Total cost as a percentage of Revenue	Total cost as a percentage of Revenue

In column one, the cost items are related to the retention and enhancement of product benefits. Some of these items or programs are undertaken regularly but a few like product improvement program may be carried out occasionally. However, the cost of these programs when measured as a percentage of the annual revenue and compared with the previous years would reflect the extra efforts the company takes to retain and boost brand loyalty. Ideally, the total cost of all programs, when analyzed column by column as a percentage of the revenue, would be useful.

The items in second column represent the company's effort to create extra value. Such actions may include the cost of offering discounts from the regular list price, special promotional offers aimed at retaining or attracting customers as well as the cost of not increasing the price over a specific period of time. Even when obliged to increase the selling price due to increasing production cost, some companies would try to assure price stability without passing it on to the customer. The items in the third column represent those actions and programs that would provide extra convenience to the customers.

Production stability would guarantee consistent supply of products and cost of establishing a system for this can be considered as part of the cost of building loyalty. So are the cost of improving and managing the channels of distribution as well managing the supply chain, including purchasing. The fourth column include programs and strategies undertaken to build and improve positive images, retain and restore the current image, and to recover the lost or negative brand images as well as corporate reputation. Such programs would include regular advertisements and promotion, public relation campaigns, sponsorships of community events, brand name changes as well as hoards of other promotion related activities that any firm would normally carry out regularly.

Brand Expenditure Outcome Audit

This audit is related to the monitoring and assessment of certain outcomes arising from the company's efforts to build and manage customer brand loyalty. The standards or measurement units may not at first seem to reflect the issues of measuring brand loyalty. However, a careful observation would prove that these measures, in fact, would reflect the level of loyalty that the customers would have built towards the brand. The table below shows some of the measures that can be monitored and compared with previous years or other standards. But, it is not necessary to monitor and assess all of them. One of the integrated brand loyalty indices would be the number of repeat purchase and its rate of growth.

Table 7: Brand Expenditure Outcome Audit

Benefit	Value	Convenience	Image
Quality (1) performance index	Overall value improvement (as if a customer)	Number of retail outlets available	Number of Ad campaigns
Product/service (2) performance index	Price inflation rate	Channel growth rate	Number of crisis and PR campaigns launched
Number of complaints logged	Average discount percentage offered	Average inventory level	Number of sales promotions
No of complaints resolved and Customer satisfaction level	The average price per unit sold (3)	Number of cities or towns served	Number of sponsorships

1. Quality index as measured by the company production or operations department; 2. Product service performance perceived and rated as a customer; and 3. Because of the various discount levels offered for different market segments or regions/seasons, an average price per unit sold such as the average room price in hotels is an important measure.

Integrated Assessment

In order to make sense out of the various assessments under the internal analysis, we may need to integrate and evaluate the various analyses using qualitative as well as quantitative techniques. Technically speaking, the level of brand loyalty as perceived by the staff associated with the brand gives us a quantifiable index as the customer brand loyalty index. Also, the brand expenditure audit provides the level of brand related expenditure made by the firm, which can be compared with some standards or historic averages. Only the last item of brand expenditure outcomes as identified in the above table needs further evaluation based on any available but appropriate standards or criteria. Here, the brand manager can undertake a subjective assessment based on the overall performance by giving a rating (on an eleven point scale, for example) for every item under the BVCI categories as shown later.

For example, under the 'benefit' category, there are four units of measurements. The quality performance index is a measure related to the outcomes of quality control process. Here, the percentage number of errors (or even success rate) or the average rate of faults detected during the production or service delivery can be considered as a valuable measure. Such a measure can be compared with an appropriate set of standards or even benchmarks or certain targets that are established as production objectives. The product and service performance index is the product success rate during product use. In the case of service product, it may represent the rate of success during production and delivery of service or consumption.

Whatever it may be, this measure is akin to customer perception and therefore should be considered as one by the respondents. Third measure is obviously the number of complaints related to the product performance. However, some of the complaints may also be related to other areas such as 'value' or 'convenience' Otherwise, this measure should be linked to the product success rate (opposites) and indirectly linked to the errors and quality control during production. The ratio of number of complaints resolved successfully to the total number of complains logged is another valuable measure in this regard.

Eventually, all the above three measures are linked to customer satisfaction. The only way to measure this item indirectly without conducting a customer perception survey is to assess the repeat purchase rate. In the end, the two quantitative measures that can be used to evaluate this category (of brand expenditure outcome on benefit) are the improvement in quality performance and the growth in repeat purchase rate. Similarly, for the 'value' category, one quantifiable measure for the brand expenditure outcome is the price inflation or the growth rate of average selling price per unit sold as a percentage of the overall revenue growth rate.

In the case of 'convenience', one integrated measure would be the sales (number of units) per retail outlet and its growth rate. If the sales volume is to grow without an apparent growth in the number of retail outlets, it may be due to other reasons. But if the ratio of growth rate is in number of units sold to the rate of growth of retail-outlets it would indicate the success of providing convenience.

As far as the 'image' factor is concerned, it is rather difficult to assess the brand loyalty effect with one specific measure. However, the total cost of advertisement and promotion campaigns as well the sponsorships is easy to determine. Also, the cost of error and the accompanied expenditure on recalling as well as regenerating the lost image can be estimated to a great degree of accuracy. The unit cost of all these image-related activities should provide a unique measure to assess the level of brand loyalty without tapping into customer perceptions. The lower the unit cost is greater is the loyalty effect. Following (matrix analysis: diagram 2) is an example how an integrated analysis can be carried out for the brand expenditure (cost) and expenditure outcome assessment. Once carried out, this can be compared with the brand performance index in table 5. The key indices shown are for the loyalty attributes of BVCI variables.

Assessment Methodology

Before an Expenditure-Outcome Matrix is constructed, it seems necessary to develop a set of appropriate indices for the two variables. Although we have seen a number of measurement units for the assessment of both the Brand Expenditure and Expenditure Outcomes in tables 6 and 7, those units themselves would not give us the necessary indices for the proposed project. The methodology for the integrative assessment involves the administration of a survey questionnaire among the senior brand management as well other relevant senior management staffs. It is similar to the Delphi technique we used in case study 3 (brand performance assessment). However, here the respondents should be senior management staff who would have some financial or budgetary responsibilities.

The data collected for the measurement units for the brand expenditure and outcome tables above may need to be circulated among the participants of this survey. The table below shows the two sets of survey questionnaire, one for the brand expenditure and other for the expenditure outcomes:

Here the two columns represents two surveys, one for the assessment of the expenditure related to the brand development and improvement programs and the other, for the assessment of the expenditure outcomes as related to the brand development and improvement programs carried out. The rate column shows the average of the (hypothetical) ratings assigned by the respondents on an eleven point scale of 0 to 10, where a rating of 5 represents neutral. The 'wgt' column represents the weighting assigned to the four different attributes of loyalty, benefit, value, convenience, and image. The weighting indicates the level of importance assigned by the researchers to the various loyalty-attributes.

Table 8: Brand Expenditure versus Expenditure Outcomes

Brand Expenditure Audit				Brand Expenditure Outcomes		
1	**Benefit-Attributes Expenditure**	**Rate**	**Wgt**	**Benefit-Attributes Related**	**Rate**	**Wgt**
A	Growth in the number of programs	6	0,30	Improvement in quality (production-related)	6	0.30
B	Quality of program implementation	7	0.30	Product performance improvement	6	0.30
C	Growth in expenditure as a % of revenue	6	0.30	Improvement in complaint resolution	6	0.30
2	**Value-Attributes Expenditure**			**Value-Attributes Related**		
A	Growth in the number of programs	6	0.20	Improvement in the overall product value	5	0.20
B	Effectiveness of programs implemented	6	0.20	Price stability as per price inflation	6	0.20
C	Growth in expenditure as % of revenue	7	0.20	Growth in the Average Unit Price	7	0.20
3	**Convenience-Attributes Expenditure**			**Convenience-Attributes Related**		
A	Growth in the number of programs	7	0.20	Growth in distribution channels	7	0.20
B	Effectiveness of program implementation	6	0.20	Growth in the areas covered (geographical)	6	0.20
C	Growth in expenditure as a % of revenue	7	0.20	Growth in the average inventory exit rate	6	0.20
4	**Image-Attributes Expenditure**			**Image-Attributes Related**		
A	Growth in the number of programs	8	0.30	Effectiveness of programs implemented	6	0.30
B	Effectiveness of programs implemented	6	0.30	Growth in the revenue or units sold	6	0.30
C	Growth in expenditure as a % of revenue	8	0.30	Overall improvement in the brand image	7	0.30

Diagram 2: Brand Expenditure – Outcome Matrix:

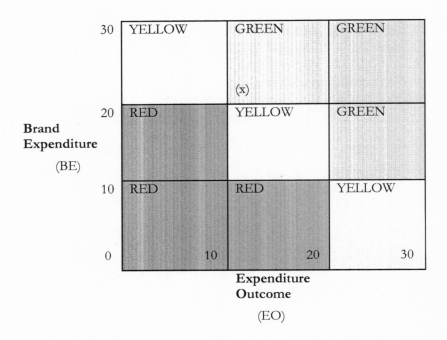

As it stands, the final score for the brand expenditure category is 20.10 and for the expenditure outcome category is 18.5. Based on a maximum score of 10 x 3 = 30 for each attribute and the assigned weights as shown, the maximum score attainable for both the categories is 30. Here, the final score for the Brand Expenditure column as a whole is 20.10 divided by 30, which is 67% and for the Expenditure Outcome column, it is 18.5 divided by 30 equal to 61.6%. This has an efficiency ratio of 61.6/67 = 91%. For our matrix analysis, the total column score of 30 is divided into three different sections with 10 scores each, so that nine different boxes can be identified to evaluate the level of effort taken to manage the brand loyalty and the related outcomes.

In the above example described, the Brand Expenditure (BE) score is 20.10 and the Expenditure Outcome (EO) score is 18.5. By placing the BE and EO coordinates in the matrix, we find the conjoining point in the Green Zone, which is satisfactory. Ideally, in order to make it highly satisfactory, it should have been in the upper left hand corner box of the green zone. Also, a composite score can be obtained by multiplying the two scores. It means, 18.5 x 20.10 = 372. This when divided by the maximum potential score of 900, we get a Brand Loyalty Development (BLDI) Index of just only 0.41 or 41%, which is obviously very low. However, for practical reasons, it may seem logical to divide the composite score by an optimum potential score such as 80% of the maximum, which is 900 x 0.80 = 720. It means 372 divided by 720 to give a BLDI of 0.516 or just over 51%. When we compare this index with the Brand performance Index of 0.71 or 71%, we can still see the apathy or management complacence towards brand loyalty management

Expenditure-Outcomes Matrix: Further Interpretation

From the table in the previous page, both columns can be evaluated independently for the four attributes of BVCI. For example, for the benefit attributes of the BE column, the total score of 19 x 0.30 =5.7 that can be compared with the total score of 20.10, which is 28.5% nearly. Similarly for the value, convenience, and image attributes are 18.4%, 19.4%, and 32.4% respectively. Obviously, firm's efforts to develop and manage brand loyalty in terms of the brand expenditure, clearly seem to have an emphasis on the image and benefit attributes (32.4% and 28.5%).

Also, surprisingly, in terms of the outcomes that may have resulted from the expenditure, the scores would also tell us something of a similar pattern. For example, as we can see from the table in the previous page, the scores of the expenditure outcomes (EO) as a percentage of the total, are 29.22%, 19.5%, 21.5%, and 31.8% for benefit, value, convenience, and image attributes respectively. There is obviously a high degree of correlation between the two sets of scores.

In conclusion, it is clear that we can now determine and evaluate some useful measures of the internal assessment and compare them with that of the external assessment in the previous chapter. The brand performance index measures the level of brand success as perceived by the brand representatives (anyone involved in the development, production, pricing and sales & marketing staffs) within the company.

In our hypothetical case, it was 0.71 or 71% success rate. The brand expenditure audit and expenditure outcome as assessed by the BE/EO expert opinion survey using the senior brand executives and the senior management staff with financial and marketing responsibilities reveals the level of company efforts in terms of expenditure as well as the outcome related to the expenditure as perceived by the management. There are of course a number of measures in this regard.

The perceived expenditure (BE) level to the potential expenditure was 67% and the perceived outcome level (EO) to the potential was only 61.6%. The overall performance of expenditure versus outcome from the BE - EO matrix was just satisfactory with a composite BLDI score of 0.516. Here, it meant only 51.6% of the optimum potential. Detailed evaluation of the matrix analysis also revealed that the deficient areas are expenditure on the improvement of value and convenience attributes in general and to some extent the improvement of product features and benefits.

13 CLM Goals and Objectives

Introduction

The purpose of the internal and external analyses carried out in the previous chapters remains to identify the appropriate brand loyalty management goals so that specific loyalty management objectives can be set. While the external analysis is aimed at assessing the level of brand loyalty as perceived by the customer, internal analysis is directed at determining the level of (as perceived by the company and brand management staff) effort undertaken to manage brand loyalty and to achieve customer retention objectives. It obviously involves assessing the customer loyalty level as perceived by the brand representatives and senior management within the company.

The Four Generic CLM Goals

These two analyses should lead to a matching process where the demand side of the loyalty is evaluated against the supply side. In someway, it is also akin to the SWOT analysis that we carry out in the strategic planning process. While internal analysis helps identify the brand strengths or weaknesses, external analysis should help identify the emerging threats and opportunities. In the end, the CLM goals are said to be determined by the entire assessment process. In fact, there are four fundamental CLM goals to be reckoned with (as shown in figure 1). These generic goals are 1) loyalty generation, 2) loyalty retention, 3) loyalty enhancement, and 4) loyalty restoration. The purpose of the whole exercise remains to determine the most appropriate goal or goals to pursue based on the internal and external analyses carried out.

Loyalty Generation

If and when the external assessment showed a general lack of brand loyalty as seen by the target customer group, obviously the company would need to start developing strategies to build and generate brand loyalty. A general lack of brand loyalty as perceived by the customer may also occur because of management's lack of awareness and therefore lack of any efforts to build customer loyalty. It may also happen due to lack of focus or emphasis, or even lack of understanding of the concept of customer loyalty or the right loyalty attributes to be created by the management.

One may question whether it is necessary to build a brand name and image in the first place. In fact, the firm may find it possible to build and generate customer brand loyalty because of the emerging opportunity. Although the brand name helps to identify and recognize the product by the customer, it does not always leads to purchases or customer recruitment. Whatever the initial objectives may be, there is a need to build or generate brand awareness if the firm is to recruit customers and generate brand loyalty if the firm is to retain customers. Therefore, the CLM goal here becomes essentially customer recruitment and loyalty generation. Most firms just opt out to undertaking fancy marketing communication campaigns to build brand or company image but fail to attend to other loyalty attributes of BVCI factors. Also, loyalty determinants or the C variables play a strategic role in generating customer brand loyalty.

Loyalty Retention

Once a firm is successful in generating brand loyalty, then the challenge becomes to retain it. Is it really necessary to have a brand name in the first place to retain the customer? After all the whole purpose of branding and loyalty generation and retention is to keep the customers that the firm has recruited. Customer recruitment is an expensive exercise but once recruited, it is not easy to retain them forever. This can only be done by generating customer loyalty and implementing loyalty retention strategies. Most brand management strategies lack any vision to foresee the emerging threats of competitions. Threats can also come from customer fatigue due to management complacency that would lead to losing the customers.

If the firm has already attained the first goal of generating customer loyalty, then the next major goal becomes to achieve loyalty retention. In simple language, it means repeat purchase because the customer is satisfied and seems to have confidence that the brand would not let him or her down. It is cheaper to retain the brand loyalty and the company reputation than restoring the lost brand image or loyalty. Firms and brand managers need to be vigilant and constantly watch for any shortcomings in the BVCI attributes as well as the loyalty determinants of five C variables.

Loyalty Enhancement

Loyalty retention strategies, in fact, should lead to enhancing or augmenting customer brand loyalty. We learned that loyalty is a bond driven by emotional attraction because of the attributes of loyalty are seen, felt and enjoyed by the customer. If generating brand loyalty is rather difficult a task, then retention can be even more difficult to attain. Customer retention as well as brand loyalty retention demands the firm to be consistent in delivering the loyalty attributes of BVCI that is characterized mainly by having to assure the last or 'continuity' variable of the 5 Cs or loyalty determinants.

However, loyalty enhancement requires more effort than just focusing on the 'continuity' variable and therefore the (the first four of the five Cs) strategic loyalty determinants should be examined within the context of the BVCI attributes. The 'commitment' factor of the loyalty determinant plays an important role in the process of loyalty augmentation or enhancement. While repeat purchases would gradually create confidence if and when the experiences turn out to be positive and satisfactory, an extra effort taken by the producer, seller or the service provider to satisfy the customer would definitely enhance loyalty. Strategically planned and implemented public relations initiatives can also help enhance brand loyalty and company reputation successfully.

Loyalty Restoration

The last of the customer loyalty management goals is to restore loyalty that the brand or firm enjoyed before. Intentionally, no firm would lose its reputation or brand loyalty but it can happen due to unavoidable circumstances or lack of vision or strategic thinking. Brand loyalty can tarnish because of operational blunders from the part of the management. When the brand image is ruined, it can also pull down the firm's reputation along with it. Accidents do happen but effective and timely communication efforts can save the brand's and firm's reputation. This is where most of the public relations campaigns are expected to play an important role.

Most often, the brand image and therefore brand loyalty tarnishes because of the complacency from the part of management. The marketing managers just ignore the emerging trends and even fail to detect the faltering brand loyalty but take it for granted that everything is running smoothly. Here, the BVCI attributes are not cared for and the strategic loyalty determinants are ignored. Only when the bottom line starts to hit red, brand managers and marketing managers would take any serious effort to look at brand loyalty. In this case, brand loyalty restoration can be considered a strategic issue rather than crisis management.

CLM Objectives

The CLM objectives are drawn from CLM goals that we have examined in the previous paragraphs. As in any objective setting process, it is important that we consider having SMART characteristics for the desired targets. At least, the objectives should be specific with realistic targets to achieve and they need to be measurable or verifiable. In the case of strategic customer loyalty management, there are two dimensions to setting CLM objectives. The first is about loyalty specific attributes (BVCI) and determinants (5Cs) and the second dimension is related to identifying specific market segments based on CLB or customer loyalty behavior that we discussed in the earlier chapters. These two dimensions are required for targeting when it comes to developing a loyalty programs and strategies for implementation as discussed in chapter 14.

Role of Loyalty Attributes and Loyalty Determinants

The internal analysis that we have carried out before should enable us to assess the deficiencies in the areas of loyalty attributes such as product benefits, value, convenience and image. We have already noted the overall attribute-driven loyalty index calculated from these BVCI variables in the earlier chapters. If the customer brand loyalty is seen to be slipping because of the weaknesses in the areas of providing product benefit, value for money, availability and convenience, or brand image, then we should be able to pinpoint the specific loyalty objective areas and set the desired targets to achieve. In other word, we can say, for example, the main cause for slipping customer loyalty (say, for example, under the loyalty retention goal) was not providing convenience due to inefficient distribution channel. And, it can be due to the inadequate level of supply, inefficient distribution network, or even product not being available to the customer on a timely manner.

Similarly, we can also look at the five loyalty determinants (or conformity, confidence, commitment, communication, and continuity factors). Although we can now assess these factors independently to identify and pinpoint the weaknesses that are causing the customer loyalty to slip, they also remain as relative variables. It means these C variables should be examined in relation to the BVCI factors of the loyalty attributes. For example, we can analyze whether the main cause for slipping loyalty is due to the weakness in the area of firm's one or two C factors such as 'conformity' and 'communication' factors related to the 'convenience' variable of the BVCI attributes. When the causes are identified and magnitudes of the cause-factors are determined, major part of the objectives setting process becomes complete.

Role of CLB-led Market Segments

What specific market segments or customer groups to target when it comes to generating, retaining, enhancing or restoring brand loyalty remains one of the main problems that is associated with Brand Loyalty Management. This is an extremely important issue as much as the identification of BVCI attributes and C determinants that we discussed in the foregoing paragraph. We have already examined the various CLB-led market segments under the key categories of benefit-seeking, value-seeking, convenience-seeking, and image-seeking groups of customers. Each of these core segments can be further divided into four sub-segments based on the 5Cs or loyalty determinants as seen in chapter 3 and 4. Next chapter describe the characteristics and benefits that these 16 CLB-led market segments can offer.

In setting the CLM objectives, therefore, we need to identify the appropriate loyalty-centered market segments seeking specific benefits from a permutation of four BVCI attributes and the five C variables (loyalty determinants) that would help achieve the CLM goals. The CLM goals are of course loyalty generation, retention, enhancement and restoration. With this in mind any reader can now brows through the benefits of the 16 market segments in chapter 14 so that relevant CLM program with specific objectives can be identified.

14 Characteristics of CLB-led Market Segments

Introduction

It is worth examining the characteristics and benefits of the CLB-led market segments that we have identified before in detail. The sixteen market segments under the four key loyalty behavior segments where each has four sub-segments with two key dimensions are examined here. This would help the reader identify appropriate CLM programs to be implemented in order to achieve the CLM goals and objectives.

Benefit-centered Loyalty Behavior Segments

1A. Guarantee of brand functionality and performance.

When a product purchase is accompanied by a warranty, certificates, and company assurance on product quality and performance etc. customers do trust and loyalty builds up. If the customer is aware of these guarantees and assured again and again during repeat purchases, then the customer's loyalty to the brand and company is said to increase enormously.

1B. Quality assurance for brand attributes and specifications

Most companies fail to inform the customers about the attributes, standards and product specifications. In some cases, the company may not have such policy to adopt standards or quality specifications. Clear and explicit quality assurance measures and national & international quality standards on products and processes such as the ISO 9000 may give the customer tremendous confidence and can boost their loyalty towards the brand as well as the company.

2A. Reliability in delivering benefits as promised.

It means the customer can rely on the brand or company reputation and image to deliver results. When the product functions as expected as well as the attributes of the product or brand deliver benefits, then the customer unconsciously begins to builds up loyalty towards the brand name and the company that manufactures it. Here, the customer takes it for granted that the product or brand would function according to the specifications, and every repeat purchase reinforces this expectation and so is the brand loyalty.

2B. Successful outcome and satisfactory brand performance

Delivering results is not just enough and the customer should be satisfied with the results. It means the product or brand should function as expected and the outcome is therefore a successful event. When the customer is satisfied with the brand performance, obviously, the customer's attachment and loyalty to the brand grows. Every successful outcome reinforces the customer loyalty behavior towards the brand.

3A. Commitment to deliver customer satisfaction

It really refers to the company's commitment to outperform the competitors. The commitment is shown not only by the high degree of product or brand quality and satisfactory marketing policies but also the services that the company performs to satisfy the customer during and after-sales episodes. Continued commitment to go for an extra mile to satisfy the customer definitely helps build customer confidence and brand loyalty.

3B. Excellence in customer service

The excellent performance of the sales and service staff driven by courtesy, attention to detail, responsiveness, and effective & appropriate complaint resolution and handling process give the customer tremendous assurance about the brand and firm that eventually leads to building loyalty.

4A. Informing brand attributes and benefits effectively

A company may be committed to deliver quality and benefits as expected by the customer but if the customer is not informed or the information techniques used are not effective, then it may give the rivals an unfair competitive advantage. The right information at the right time and delivered through appropriate media may help customers establish trust and confidence leading to building enhanced loyalty behavior. Effective communication with the customer also involves enabling the customers to interact and exchange views about the product functions and benefits with the firm. All these would increase the chance to building and enhancing loyalty behavior towards a brand.

4B. Effective packaging and branding of benefit attributes

This is about packaging the above characteristics and developing a powerful brand image. It means shedding light on matters such as company's commitment to quality and specifications, reliability and successful outcomes as expressed by customers, evidence of delivering customer satisfaction and excellent customer service etc. Effective branding can help achieve these objectives. The brand image thus created in the customers mind should be able to link the above attributes to the product benefits so that they begin to build loyalty towards the brand.

Value-centered Loyalty Behavior Segments

1A. Value for money assurance

This is another form of guarantee where the company assures the customer to provide a reasonable value as measured in terms of product price. Perceived value may be expressed in terms of enhanced quality and performance as compared to the rival brands or simply the lowest or reasonable price in the market for a comparatively good product under specific circumstances. Such assurance when realized continuously by the customer may lead to building brand loyalty.

1B. Guarantee of price stability

Continued value is often measured by price stability. Product improvement can cost the firm over a period of time but transferring such cost to customer should be matched by perceived value of the brand. Therefore, company policy and guarantee on price stability and commitment to justify and effectively inform the customer any price increase in advance may help to boost brand loyalty.

2A. Delivering value to customers

The promise of value for money is often not taken for granted by the customers until they realize the value through a purchase experience. Of course, continued purchase depends on delivering that value as perceived by the customer. Since the value can be measured by monetary units or otherwise, companies need to research the customer perceived values and what they perceive it as having value. If the customer perceives the brand as having value time and again during repeat purchases, it can help build loyalty behavior.

2B. Price stability in practice

As in the case of perceived value, promise of price stability is not enough. Companies should deliver price stability over a period of time. Customers do compare often the current price with past prices and competitors prices before committing to a repurchase. Since most customers are very much price sensitive, they can be easily driven to switch brands if perceived product as having less value over a period of time. Price inflation or the rate at which the retail price changes compared to the unit cost is a good measure to watch out. Without doubt, price stability can help boost confidence and brand loyalty in the long run.

3A. Making sincere efforts to enhance value

This involves any effort that the company makes to enhance or add value to the customer. It is not only the product value in the form of benefits but also other factors such as providing price value by means of promotional offers or convenience (home delivery) without additional cost as well as creating psychological benefits through brand identity. Any effort or actions and services provided by the firm and when perceived by the customer as 'beyond the call of duty' can enhance value and cause loyalty behavior to increase

3B. Delivering customer satisfaction through value-attribute

Any actions that the company takes to create and enhance value as seen above can lead to generate customer satisfaction over a period of time. Here the customer perceives the brand as having some value that is relatively more than the rival brands when compared against competitors' offers during repeat purchases. Higher degree of perceived satisfaction thus generated can create brand loyalty.

4A. Informing customer the value attributes convincingly

Although the firm is committed to deliver value and price stability as expected, the customer may not be informed or the information techniques used may not be effective. It may give the rivals an unfair competitive advantage. The right information at the right time about the value of the brand and delivered through appropriate media may help customers establish trust and confidence leading to building enhanced loyalty behavior. Such information techniques may include also timely sales promotions.

4B. Informing customers effectively the price stability factor

The customer should be informed about the above characteristics such as company's commitment to providing value and price stability as evidenced by successful value outcomes. Any effort to maximize by over-pricing needs to be balanced by quality enhancement and effective communication. This would also include effective communication with the customer enabling to interact and exchange views and ideas about product or brand values and price. These would increase the chance to building and enhancing customer brand loyalty.

Convenience-centered Loyalty Behavior Segments

1A. Promise of efficient and effective distribution channels

The company policy should be clear here on establishing and maintaining an efficient and effective distribution channel. This includes the intermediaries and retail locations or even courier or home delivery systems in the case of e-commerce. Moreover, it is also important to guarantee channels for after-sales services, including complaint handling. Such policies and commitment would help boosting customer confidence and trust leading to loyalty behavior. Continued commitment indeed encourages repeat purchase and brand loyalty.

1B. Promise of product availability

Product availability means guarantee of supply to all retail locations or whenever the customer needs it. The company may have a reliable distribution system but can fail to guarantee supplies because of logistics or slacking production levels. If the customer can be convinced that the company is committed to guarantee supplies as well as arrangements for after-sales services, it can help boost customer confidence and brand loyalty.

2A. Assuring sales and services in convenient locations

A promise may not mean anything if the company cannot deliver. It means the channels of distribution and arrangements for after-sales service should be in place in practice. For example, a hotel guest should have a chain of properties when she or he needs it in a specific location as promised. Of course, these arrangements should also be convenient (convenient retail location or convenient time of home delivery). When the customer sees this in practice, loyalty behavior can be enhanced.

2B. Availability of products and services

This simply means the customer has access to retail or other outlets and the product supply is also available when needed. Non-availability of product or outlets for services is one of the guaranteed causes of brand switching. If a hotel guest cannot find a room for a night at a promised location (although there may be a hotel property), he or she will be forced to go and find another brand and who knows the guest may never come back again in the future. Also, a dissatisfied customer may need an outlet or an arrangement to complain (a complaining customer is always seem to be more loyal than the non-complaining one). Since the customer takes it for granted that the product and services are always available when needed, continued non-availability can harm brand loyally.

3A. Effective management of the supply chain and channels

This is an extension to the above characteristic. Every aspects of the supply chain process is monitored and managed to avoid any system breakdown. In some cases such as home delivery, the promise of punctuality becomes an issue but companies can compensate the customer for any broken promises. Any extra efforts made to satisfy the customers are often rewarded with continued brand loyalty.

3B. Delivering the product to customer even in Timbuktu

Here, the company takes extra efforts and measures to bring the product and services to customers even if the regular channels are not available or ineffective due to system failures. Spare parts and service crew when breakdown occurs on the road, an English-speaking doctor when in China, money or checks to replace the lost Travelers Check while on holidays are some of the example how companies try to deliver their promises out of their ways. These actions obviously would help boost the brand loyalty.

4A. Informing the customer effectively the brand availability

Sometimes, the customer is not aware of the retail outlets that stocks company brands or even the locations of the outlets. Also, since the customer takes it for granted that the company's products are available when required any problems with the delivery of supplies should be effectively informed. So is any alternative arrangement that the company makes to supply the goods. Specially, this is true with mobile customers who may find it difficult to get the brand or locate a seller. Effective communication with the customer in this regard would definitely enhance customer brand loyalty.

4B. Informing any special delivery arrangements effectively

Customer may not be aware of some of the special delivery or service arrangements that the company has in place. Home delivery of food, complaint handling through the Internet, lost check replacement through local representative etc. is some of the examples where companies make special arrangements. But these need to be informed effectively to the target customers so that they could use when needed most. Offering these facilities without customers' knowledge is a cost burden with no returns. Moreover, availability of these facilities can help enhance the existing brand loyalty.

Image-centered Loyalty Behavior Segments

1A. Assurance of prestige, identity and exclusivity

Brand image and firm's reputations can provide some psychological benefits such as prestige, exclusivity, and social identity etc. If the customers are convinced that brand image or firm's reputation is guaranteed to give them such attributes, then they can be wooed to buy them. If the firm continues to provide that guarantee of perceived image, then the customers may even show loyalty behavior towards the brand. Designer labels, names such as Harrods of London, luxury brands such as Ferrari are some of the top of the range example that assure to provide these attributes and therefore brand loyalty.

1B. Creating a sense of reliability via brand image

Brands and company images also provide some sense of reliability to customers. If the company can guarantee to deliver quality and performance through the brand image thus created, then the customer can show loyalty towards the brands. Brands do have the power to communicate with the customers and repeat purchase experiences can reinforce the promise of quality and reliability leading to enhancing loyalty behavior.

2A. Delivering the brand promise as perceived by customers

Keeping the brand promise by delivering as expected by the customers will definitely boost the confidence and loyalty. An effective branding strategy should be linked to product or brand performance leading to successful outcome so that the customer can build confidence and attachment to the brand.

2B. Brand performance and reinforcement of confidence

Repeat purchases by the customer demands repeat performance again and again. Every time the brand satisfies the customer with successful outcomes, confidence is reinforced and customer loyalty towards the brand is said to grow. This is what we see as the power of branding.

3A. Enhancing the brand image and company reputation

This process is aimed at retaining and enhancing the current positive brand image and company reputation. In order to do this, companies should try to deliver beyond the customer expectations in every sense. Of course, these actions should be linked to the brand and company image through effective communication techniques such as advertising so that brand loyalty can be enhanced. Most firms do engage in this practice but fail to deliver other attributes.

3B. Protecting brand image and reputation

Protecting and retaining the brand image or a firm's reputation is as important as the firm's attempt to create them. Unexpected events leading to major product-service failures or adverse impacts arising from the use or consumption of the product can badly hurt the firm's reputation and the brand image. A fail-proof system of production and service delivery coupled with proven quality control systems can reduce the probability of such events occurring. Proactive strategies can be developed to prevent and protect any major disasters from occurring and such actions may help build customer loyalty in the long run when communicated effectively.

4A. Creating the link between the brand image and benefits

The positive image thus created for the brand and company should be implanted in the minds of the target market group in particular and the public in general using effective communication methods and tools. Whenever the customer thinks about the brand name or company name, he or she should be able to relate to the benefits and positive attributes that the company has created in the customers mind. The whole thing should be an emotional episode leading to creating and enhancing loyalty behavior towards the brand and the firm.

4B. Managing the brand image and reputation when in crisis

The last thing the company should be able to do is to manage any crisis situation that would arise from either product and service failures and breakdowns or adverse impacts of product consumption or utilization. This is where the company requires the work of an effective public relations (PR) manager. Honesty, openness and promptness remain the major characteristics of an effective PR strategy. The target customers should be well informed about the crisis and its causes promptly. Actions should also be taken to compensate for any damages fairly and such actions need to be effectively and unambiguously informed if customer loyalty is to be restored.

15 CLM Programs: Development and Implementation

Introduction

The CLM or customer loyalty management programs simply refer to the alternative strategies we would implement in order to achieve loyalty objectives and therefore customer retention. Such measures are essentially aimed at managing customer brand loyalty strategically but often may include the usual loyalty programs that firms carry out without any strategic framework. The frequent flier membership program offering bonus air miles by airlines is a good example to note. However, since these schemes are often carried out without any links to the strategic brand loyalty management goals, such programs becomes mere sales promotional tools than a loyalty strategy.

The core purpose of any CLM programs is to facilitate and therefore linked to achieving the brand loyalty management goal and objectives that we discussed in the previous chapters. Any such programs recommended should be aimed at achieving one or more of the generic CLM goals eventually. The basic CLM goals are loyalty generation, retention, enhancement and restoration. And the CLM objectives should therefore have some targets to be achieved that are related to identifying the required BVCI attributes and the five Cs determinants within the specific target group (s) of customers derived from the CLB-led market segmentation.

The key CLB-led market segments are Benefit-seeking, value-seeking, convenience-seeking, and image-seeking customer groups. But, it should be reminded that these four groups can be further divided into a total of 16 segments.

Developing CLM or Customer Loyalty Initiatives

Based on the specific requirement of the CLM goals, brand managers can formulate strategies or programs in order to achieve the CLM objectives. Even frequent user programs as seen in the hotel or airline sectors can be considered as CLM programs when such programs are developed as part of the overall strategic brand loyalty management activity. In other words, these programs should be aimed at achieving such goals as customer loyalty creation or retention. Ideally all loyalty management programs can be seen as having something to do with boosting brand attributes of benefit, value, convenience or image. If, for example, these core benefits of the product are seen as lacking by the target group of customers, any strategy or project aimed at improving the product benefits and performance would become a CLM program.

Simply said, creating value, improving product quality, building or improving the channels of distribution, ensuring product availability, and even launching a PR campaign to restore the ruined image all can be CLM programs. Not to mention the most talked about Customer Relationship Management programs.

We have already examined how the BVCI variables are linked to the customer loyalty attributes that remain the driving forces behind brand loyalty generation, retention, enhancement, and restoration. The BVCI variables stand for benefit, value, convenience, and image attributes that again correspond to the four marketing mix variables of product, price, place, and promotion respectively. This therefore explains us how important is it to offer the BVCI attributes as expected by the target customer group if the brand is to enjoy their loyalty. Since all BVCI attributes would lead to providing customer satisfaction, it is of paramount importance that we deliver benefit, value, convenience, and image through various loyalty programs and not merely by popular CRM initiatives. In fact, CRM programs can be considered as related to the last attribute of the BVCI variables because it involves communication.

The 5 C-variables of conformity, confidence, commitment, communication, and continuity are also important here. Although these C-variables do not play a part in generating or improving customer loyalty directly, they do influence the loyalty attributes of BVCI variables directly, most importantly, in the development of CLB-driven market segments. Segmentation does help to identify and target specific groups of customers and therefore in setting objectives of the customer loyalty initiatives or CLM programs. In the meantime, any initiatives aimed at improving the C-variables (linked to any of the BVCI variables) can also constitute a CLM program.

Some of the examples of CLM programs or Customer Loyalty Initiatives are product improvement (developing and or improving the actual and augmented product components), branding strategy, any programs to create value (including price stability), improving the channels of distribution (including guaranteed availability), and image or reputation building and restoration programs (including PR campaigns to restore ruined image). As we can see, all these programs should be strategic in nature and not merely a tactical tool. Moreover, all such projects are directly linked to the marketing mix variables.

Table 9: C-Variable versus BVCI Attributes Matrix

	Benefit	Value	Convenience	Image
Conformity	3	4	5	4
Confidence	4	5	5	5
Commitment	3	4	3	5
Communication	5	4	5	6

Initially, critical areas for CLM program can be detected using some form of assessment such as rating of the current level of provision or delivery of BVCI attributes that are specific to the C-variables as shown table 9.

The current level of loyalty determinants as defined by the C-variables related to the CVCI attributes can be rated based on the research and analysis carried periodically to assess the current situation. This can be done using a 7-point scale where anything less than a rating of four can be considered deficient that would warrant an appropriate CLM program or programs. Obviously, in the above table, conformity-benefit, commitment-benefit, and commitment-convenience are seen as deficient and therefore would require some attention to improve the level of loyalty attributes in these areas.

Moreover, it is also worth reminding the advantages of re-visiting the sixteen (four x four) CLB-led market segments that we examined in the earlier chapters. Understanding the key characteristics of these market segments as expected by the target customers would be useful when it comes to identifying and developing any CLM programs or initiatives. The following can be considered as some of the examples of Customer Brand Loyalty Initiatives: programs that guarantees or enhances 1) brand attributes, 2) product functionality in delivering benefits, 3) brand performance in terms of realized outcomes, and 4) quality (assurance as well as delivering quality and satisfaction to the customer).

Implementing and Evaluating CLM Initiatives

Once a CLM program is initiated, designed, developed and prioritized for implementation, an action plan should be in place so that necessary tasks can be determined along with the resource allocation plan. Such an action plan should also include roles and responsibilities of the agencies and people who would be involved in the project. It is important to note the CLM programs or initiatives should be strategic in nature and therefore could last for sometime. This requires the brand managers or customer loyalty managers to focus on the resource allocation and to budget appropriately. A clear set of milestones and time schedules to achieve the desired project targets needs to be established. Some initiatives can last for years as in the case of loyalty card programs. Here. The progress and any obstacles in the smooth running of the program need to be monitored carefully so that the success can be evaluated.

Some examples of specific targets to be achieved can be retaining the existing level of frequent customers through a strategic CLM initiative that may or may not have a loyalty card program. Logic and common sense would tell us why should a customer keeps on buying a brand even if there is no immediate bonuses such as extra points linked to the purchase that can be redeemed. It is worth noting that loyalty card based bonus points offer only one thing to the customer that is some sort of value attributes. Other attributes of the BVCI variables that we have examined can also build customer loyalty that we often tend to ignore. Therefore, when it comes to tracking the success, we need to pay attention to the final outcomes that we have set as target that is in this case the retention of a specific level of frequent customers and other relevant outcomes.

These other outcomes may be related to the BVCI attributes that the proposed CLM program could have intended to realize. For example, it could have been a convenience-related attributes of the third C-variable. If this convenience-related attribute were to be providing Internet booking facility, for example, by a traditional independent hotel in Scotland to its customers, it would have seemed possible to retain the current frequent customer level. However, such a CLM related program would involve constant quality control process to assess the smooth functioning of the system in addition to setting up the system in the first place.

Monitoring and evaluation of the CLM initiatives therefore requires us to first examine the determined CLM goal such as loyalty retention or even loyalty restoration. Next step would be to look at the specific CLM objectives such as which BVCI attributes to be developed as well as targets as to what level these need to be achieved and what specific customer groups need to be aimed at targeting. Once the measurement units are identified and determined for CLM goals and objectives, the last steps would be to set up the time schedule and the budget targets for implementing the CLM initiative. The effectiveness of the CLM initiative would therefore rest on how successfully the program was implemented (on time and within budget) and successfully and whether the program helped achieve the CLM goals and objectives.

Endnote

The title of the book, perhaps, could have driven most of the readers to believe that this was another book on loyalty card programs or most publicized topics such as the CRM. After having read the book, however, any reader should have realized the importance of the materials covered. At first, some six years ago when the idea of writing this book was conceived, the author thought of titling the book as Brand Loyalty Management Strategy. In essence, it is this topic that the book was intended to cover. But, as the work progressed, author was able to realize a much broader context within which the concept of brand loyalty management lies. In fact, it covers the whole marketing philosophy and the concept of marketing and customer orientations. The sub-title the book, 'Managing Brand Loyalty and Customer Retention', should indicate the importance of some of the strategic issues that are focused in the book.

As for the title of the book 'Loyalty Marketing', one should understand the author's concept of customer loyalty as a 'product' in itself. Along with a lengthy description and explanation of customer loyalty, author sees customer loyalty towards a brand or firm as involving another exchange process that takes place in parallel. This is in addition to the normal exchanges of goods and services for money between the seller and the buyer. However, the seller who expects the buyer to show brand loyalty does not often offer anything in return. What is expected by the buyer would be some form of reciprocal loyalty by the seller.

This reciprocal loyalty is seen as the seller's promise of conformity to quality, building confidence in delivering the promise, committing to deliver beyond customer expectation, and communicating these factors effectively. Also these attributes of reciprocal loyalty are related to creating product benefit, value, convenience, and positive image for the brand in question. These are known as BVCI (benefit, value, convenience, and image) attributes.

Based on these BVCI attributes that the different customers would be seeking at different level, author also ventures into developing a model for market segmentation. This is done by using four C variables called loyalty determinants; conformity, confidence, commitment, and communication attributes that the seller or producer has to offer in addition to the product or service package.

Another important element of the book is the techniques that are used to assess the level of customer loyalty and the degree of effort taken by the firm or brand managers to generate or protect the brand loyalty.

It is argued that the customer loyalty to a brand slopes up at the beginning to reach maturity or stability and then declines as the loyalty diminishes over a period of time. This is akin to a product life cycle curve and therefore calls it the loyalty life cycle (LLC). The author also takes the liberty to measure customer brand loyalty based on the level of perceived BVCI attributes. In the meantime, by assessing the perceived level of loyalty by the customer and the effort taken by the firm, it is possible to match them and formulate a loyalty management strategy.

A loyalty management strategy is expected to have four generic goals; loyalty generation, loyalty enhancement, loyalty retention, and protection or restoration of customer loyalty. Objectives of brand loyalty management and customer retention are aimed at achieving these goals but remain specific with measurable targets. Any strategies in the form of programs and projects may involve loyalty management strategies. Programs such as CRM and loyalty cards and frequent customer bonuses may be considered as akin to such strategies but they would fail in terms of strategic dimension. Unfortunately, such programs are implemented with short-term vision and they fall mainly into the category of sales promotion campaigns. The book provides a model for understanding the nature of loyalty attributes and to assess such attributes so that a strategic framework to manage customer brand loyalty can be constructed.

It is however important to note that customer loyalty as a 'commodity' or 'product' requires the same effort to generate and promote it as the actual product itself would demand. This is what the author meant by loyalty marketing.

Appendix A

Loyalty Assessment: Methodology and Survey Instruments

The characteristics (described in chapter 13) of the CLB-led market segments make it easier to develop survey instruments for measuring brand loyalty intensity objectively. Based on the characteristics described, the author has constructed two instruments for each of the 16 market segments. For every C variable (conformity, confidence, commitment, and communication), four loyalty determinant criteria have been established based on the four loyalty attributes (product benefit, product value, product convenience, and product image). These have been identified as follows:

- Conformity: conformity-benefit (C1-B), conformity-value (C1-V), conformity-convenience (C1-C), and conformity-image (C1-M).

- Confidence: confidence-benefit (C2-B), confidence-value (C2-V), confidence-convenience (C2-C), and confidence-image (C2-M).

- Commitment: commitment-benefit (C3-B), commitment-value (C3-V), commitment-convenience (C3-C), and commitment-image (C3-M).

- Communication: communication-benefit (C4-B), communication-value (C4-V), communication-convenience (C4-C), and communication-image (C4-M).

The intensity of loyalty is measured by the four loyalty behaviors identified before. These are benefit-centered, value-centered, convenience-centered, and image-centered behaviors and therefore measured vertically. The benefit-centered CLB is the sum of C1-B, C2-B, C3-B, and C4-B and the value-centered CLB is the sum of C1-V, C2-V, C3-V, and C4-V. Similarly, convenience-centered and image-centered columns can be measured by adding the values of C1-C, C2-C, C3-C, and C4-C and C1-M, C2-M, C3-M, and C4-M respectively.

In order to determine the total intensity of customer brand loyalty, the sum of the vertical columns can be weighted according to the pre-determined weights of the market segments. A pilot study (case study 1) should be able to help identify the weights for each of the C variables of conformity, confidence, convenience, and communication. The following table shows the characteristics of the determinant factors and potential measurement instruments for the first sub-segment, C1-B:

Measuring Benefit-centered Loyalty Behavior

Sub-segment of C1-B (Conformity-Benefit)

Characteristics	Instruments
Guarantee of brand attributes, functionality, and performance.	I would continue to buy a specific brand if it is guaranteed to deliver quality in terms of the core benefits, attributes and performance.
Quality assurance and product specifications and standards etc.	I would continue to buy a specific brand if I am convinced that the producer or seller has provided product and service standards, specifications, and quality assurance etc.

The measurement tools are, of course, survey instruments, which can be modified and added according to the circumstances. For example, 'service' and the producer by 'service provider' can replace the word product or even brand. The assessment objectives, however, remain the same and should reflect the characteristics in the left-hand column.

For measurement, rating on a scale of 0 to 10 (as in LIKERT scale) can be used requesting the respondents to show their agreement or disagreement to the statement. An average rating of 5 would indicate the respondent's indifference to the characteristics defined by the statement. A rating of 0 would indicate total disagreement and 10 would show total agreement. In this case, the total maximum score is 20 for the Conformity-Benefit (C1-B) sub-segment The following tables show the characteristics and instruments of loyalty measurement for the rest of the C variables; confidence, commitment, and communication that are related to the benefit CLB.

Sub-segment of C2-B (Confidence-Benefit)

Characteristics	Instruments
Reliability in delivering attributes and benefits.	I would continue to buy a specific brand if I am convinced that it would deliver benefits as promised according to specifications.
Successful outcome and Satisfactory performance.	I would continue to buy a specific brand if it performs satisfactorily as expected.

Sub-segment of C3-B (Commitment-Benefit)

Characteristics	Instruments
Highly committed to deliver customer (going an extra mile) satisfaction.	I would continue to buy a product or brand if I am convinced that the producer and or seller is committed to providing customer satisfaction.
Excellent customer service during all stages (including after-sale) of customer encounters	I would continue to buy a specific brand or patronize a specific business if I am convinced that company and staff are committed to provide excellent customer service during and after sales.

Sub-segment of C4-B (Communication-Benefit)

Characteristics	Instruments
Highly committed to informing the customer effectively about the benefits and attributes & specifications.	I would continue to buy a specific brand if I am convinced that the company is committed to informing the product specifications, attributes, and benefits unambiguously.
Effectively informing the customer about the above factors (other three C variables)	I would continue to buy a specific brand if the company communicates with the customer clearly and effectively about the other three Cs related to benefit attribute and their implications.

The measurement objectives for the first C variable, Conformity, as related to the first loyalty attribute of product benefits are to assess how important is it to assure the customer the product specification and quality standards. As seen above, every C variable has two survey instruments with a maximum potential score of 80 as the CLB intensity for the benefit-centered behavior in total.

The Confidence variable on the other hand demands reliability and confidence in performance. It means customers would like to see actual delivery of company promises in terms of specifications and quality standards. The product or brand is only reliable when it delivers as promised. Here, the measurement objectives are to assess the brand performance as perceived by the customer together with customer satisfaction.

The third C variable is about Commitment to deliver the best and enhance customer satisfaction. The characteristics of this variable that are related to the attributes of product benefits are of course the company's commitment to go an extra mile to offer the best of product/brand benefits as well as customer satisfaction. The measurement objectives reflect these factors.

Effective communication plays an important role in informing the product features and benefits as well the company's effort to deliver quality and performance. The last C variable, Communication, as related to the attributes of product benefits to make sure that the customers are well-informed and therefore the objectives of measurement are to assess the image and effectiveness of communication.

Measuring Value-centered Loyalty Behavior

The table below shows the characteristics and the instruments to measure the intensity of every sub-segment of the value-centered behavior group. As above, the maximum scores for the value-centered loyalty behavior is also measured as 20 x 4 or 80.

Sub-segment of C1-V (Conformity-Value)

Characteristics	Instruments
Value for money assurance.	I would continue to buy a specific brand if I am convinced that it come with (firm's policy) value assurance.
Guarantee of price stability.	I would continue to buy a specific brand if I am convinced that it comes with a price stability assurance.

The conformity variable (determinant) of value-centered loyalty emphasizes assurance and guarantee that are related to the product or brand value. The concept of value for money does not always refer to low or affordable price but can bear other meanings such as the quality versus price or how much the product or brand is worth. If the company assures that the customer will get the best value in terms of quality and price, then the objective becomes to assess the customer perception on this assurance. Similarly, another factor that may determine the value attribute is the price stability of the brand over a period of time.

Here, the measurement objective would be to assess the level of company assurance on price stability as perceived by the customers. There are two instruments therefore to measure the intensity of loyalty with regards to the conformity variable of the value-centered brand loyalty behavior.

Similarly, for the confidence variable as related to the value-centered loyalty behavior, there are two instruments. The confidence variable refers to building confidence by being reliable in delivering the brand promise. The measurement objectives here are to assess whether the company managed to deliver its promises in providing value for money as well as price stability.

Sub-segment of C2-V (Confidence-Value)

Characteristics	Instruments
Delivering value to customers.	I would continue to buy a specific brand if I am convinced that the brand offers comparable value.
Delivering Price stability.	I would continue to buy a specific brand if I am convinced that the brand's price has been relatively stable.

Commitment to give value is the next sub-segment. The customer wouldn't be satisfied with just delivering the promise. He or she would want more in terms of performance as promised as well as beyond expectation. Here, they would like the product or brand to offer additional value or the company to make an effort to enhance value such as free repair and maintenance or warranty and free insurance for one year when purchasing a car, for example. Or, it could be some extra features or attributes at no cost. Here again, there are two instruments to measure the commitment factors. One is aimed at assessing whether company takes sincere effort to enhance brand value as perceived by the customer and the other is to assess the overall level of perceived satisfaction.

Sub-segment of C3-V (Commitment-Value)

Characteristics	Instruments
Making sincere efforts to enhance value.	I would continue to buy a specific brand if I am convinced that the company takes sincere effort to enhance brand value with additional attributes.
Providing perceived value & satisfaction.	I would continue to buy a specific brand if I perceive the product or service package as having exceptional value.

Sub-segment of C4-V (Communication-Value)

Characteristics	Instruments
Informing the values convincingly, including sales promotions.	I would continue to buy a specific brand if I am convinced that company has been successful in effectively communicating the value.
Effectively reaching and informing the price stability and value.	I would continue to buy a specific brand if the producer or seller firm inform the customer about the price changes in advance with justification

As for the sub-segments of the communication variable related to the value-centered loyalty behavior, the objectives of measurement are to assess how good the company tried to inform the customers about the brand value and price stability that are related to the offer. Informing the customers about the value aspects as well as the monetary value, including sales promotion campaigns, require to be convincing as well as being persuasive. So is the case of price stability over a period of time. Also, factual information needs to be provided on a timely basis.

Measuring Convenience-centered Loyalty Behavior

As above, there are eight instruments here, two for each of the C variables as related to the attributes of product convenience. For the sub-segments of the conformity variable as related to convenience attributes, the issue is again company assurance on providing convenience. It means promising effective channels of distribution and product availability when and where the customers need them. Therefore, the objectives of measurement are to assess the effectiveness of these promises and assurance.

Sub-segments of C1-C (Conformity-Convenience)

Characteristics	Instruments
Promise of efficient & effective channels of distribution.	I would continue to buy a specific brand if I am convinced that the firm is committed to maintaining an effective system of distribution channel.
Promise of product availability.	I would continue to buy a specific brand if I am convinced that the firm is committed to guarantee and assure product supply.

However, the promises and assurances are not just adequate. Customers would like to see them in practice so that their confidence can be built. The sub-segments of the second C variable, confidence, as related to the attributes of convenience make sure that the company has guaranteed channels of distribution and retail locations as well as the brand is available when needed. Therefore the two measurement instruments are designed to assess the success of availability and distribution as perceived by the customers.

Sub-segment of C2-C (Confidence-Convenience)

Characteristics	Instruments
Convenient sales & service locations and outlets.	I would continue to buy a specific brand if the company is committed to and providing an effective distribution channels (adequate and convenient retail outlets).
Product availability	I would continue to buy a specific brand if I am convinced that it would be available when I need it.

The third C variable, commitment, as related to the attributes of convenience (related to the product/brand) that expresses the company's desire to provide total customer satisfaction with regards to the effectiveness of distribution and logistics as well product availability. It is about the company's sincere effort to manage the supply chain effectively and provide total satisfaction to customer by making the product or brand available even in difficult locations. The objectives of measurement are to assess the achievement of these attributes as perceived by the customers.

Sub-segment of C3-C (Commitment-Convenience)

Characteristics	Instruments
Sincere effort to assure an effective supply chain system.	I would continue to buy a specific brand if I am convinced that the company takes sincere effort to make the distribution system work effectively.
Delivering the product to customer even in Timbuktu.	I would continue to buy a specific brand if the company seems to take an extra effort to supply and deliver the brand, including abroad and unusual locations.

Sub-segment of C4-C (Communication-Convenience)

Characteristics	Instruments
Effectively informing the customer about product availability as well as locations.	I would continue to buy a specific brand if I am convinced that company is committed to communicate about the supplies, availability & locations successfully.
Effectively informing customer any special features such as home delivery, services abroad etc.	I would continue to buy a specific brand if the company attempts to inform the customer about any special services and supply arrangements that are available regularly and occasionally, including abroad.

The last C variable as related to the attributes of product convenience is about communication. The company may have assurance and guarantees as well as good performance in delivering the promises but customer needs to be informed. If the attributes of convenience and their effectiveness are not communicated to the customer convincingly, all the efforts the company makes in this regards become useless. The objectives of measurement here are to assess whether the above matters have been informed effectively as perceived by the customer.

Measuring Image-centered Loyalty Behavior

In order to assess the image-led customer brand loyalty behavior, we have again eight instruments that are assigned to each of the C variable: conformity, confidence, convenience, and communication. The conformity variable related to the attributes of product benefits refers to the assurance what the brand image would bring such as the psychological benefits (for example, prestige) as well as the communication benefits of linking the brand image to product benefits and atttributes. The instruments here are designed to assess those effects as perceived by the customer.

Sub-segment of C1-M (Conformity-Image)

Characteristics	Instruments
Assurance of prestige, identity and exclusivity (Harrods, London).	I would continue to buy a product if I am convinced that the company reputation and brand image promise the customer an identity, prestige and exclusivity etc.
Creating a sense of reliability & quality via brand image.	I would continue to buy a product if I am convinced that the company reputation and brand image are guaranteed to provide quality and a sense of reliability. .

Sub-segment of C2-M (Confidence-Image)

Characteristics	Instruments
Delivering the brand promise as customer perceived.	I would continue to buy a brand if it as well as the firm delivers the promise as expected.
Brand performance as expected that reinforces customer confidence.	I would continue to buy a brand if its performance reinforces customer confidence with successful outcomes or experiences.

The second C variable of confidence related to the attributes of product or brand image is said to provide reliability in delivering the brand image and brand expectations. The objectives of measurement are therefore aimed at assessing the customer perceived brand image and its benefits and attributes, both psychological and tangible.

The enhancement and protection of the positive image and reputation are the main characteristics of the third C variable of image that is related to the attributes of brand image. The firms' efforts to enhance and protect the brand image by linking to its beneficial features and attributes as well as projecting a positive image are said to help boost loyalty. The measurement objectives are therefore to assess the customer perception of these elements.

Sub-segment of C3-M (Commitment-Image)

Characteristics	Instruments
Enhancing the brand image and company reputation.	I would continue to buy a brand if I am convinced that the company continues to take sincere effort to retain and enhance the brand image and company reputation.
Protecting brand image & reputation.	I would continue to buy a brand if the company takes an extra effort to protect and retain the current good brand image and reputation

Sub-segment of C4-M (Communication-Image)

Characteristics	Instruments
Creating the link between the brand and product benefits and other attributes with communication	I would continue to buy a brand if I am convinced that the company reputation and brand image reflect the overall product attributes and benefits, including value and convenience etc.
Managing the brand image & reputation when in crisis.	I would continue to buy a brand if the company honestly and openly informs me about the brand image crisis and takes actions to resolve the problems.

The last C variable that is related to the attributes of product or brand image is the communication. The branding strategy and the communication technique used to create brand awareness and equity as well as loyalty is all extremely important for the company. If the brand image is to be ruined either by failure to perform or due to external circumstances, then the companies' effort to recover the brand image is also important for restoring customer loyalty. The two instruments of this section are designed to assess the effectiveness of these actions as perceived by the customer.

Appendix B: Case Study 1

Determining the weights of loyalty attributes (Benefit-value-convenience-image or BVCI) and the loyalty determinants (4 C variables) of a specific market segment remains a prerequisite to measuring the intensity or level of customer brand loyalty. For this purpose, a preliminary study was conducted in the university town of BILKENT (home to one of the largest hypermarket in the capital) in the outskirt of Ankara, Turkey. The participants for the survey were first vetted for suitability as the potential market segment for a specific line of product, instant coffee. It should be reminded that the BILKENT residents were considered rather sophisticated and brand conscious customers with an above average purchasing power.

Over a period of just three months, four samples of 100 willing respondents were asked to rate the questionnaire. The respondent's age ranged from 16 to 56. BILKENT residents were rather image conscious and predominantly younger people. However, visitors to the town come from all walks of life from in and around Ankara. The tables below show the percentage breakdown of the scores of loyalty attributes and loyalty determinants for three different age groups as well as the average percentages for the two.

Scores of the Loyalty Attributes as Perceived by the Respondents

Age Groups	Benefit	Value	Convenience	Image
16 – 29	23%	19%	25%	34%
30 – 45	29%	23%	28%	20%
46 – 65	29%	27%	28%	15%
Average	27%	23%	27%	23%

The table above refers to the loyalty attributes and the customer perception of what attributes would generate customer loyalty. The table below, on the other hand, refers to the loyalty determinants and the customer perception about what criteria would determine customer loyalty.

Scores of the Loyalty Determinants as Perceived by the Respondents

Age Groups	Conformity	Confidence	Commitment	Communication
16 – 29	23%	25%	23%	24%
30 – 45	23%	29%	24%	23%
46 – 65	23%	30%	28%	25%
Average	23%	28%	25%	24%

The above tables show the percentages of the individual scores to the total scores along the columns and rows. Obviously the four columns are the loyalty attributes columns of brand benefit, brand value, brand convenience and brand image. The rows are the C variables or loyalty determinants of conformity, confidence, commitment and communication (although shown as columns in the above table). First the collected questionnaires were separated based on the three age groups and the individual scores of every survey instruments totaled and an average score was obtained. A single average score for every instrument was obtained before they were again added along the four columns and rows in order to get 8 single scores as the sum.

Therefore, the individual scores as a percentage to the total score along the columns and rows are shown above. The first table shows the percentage scores of the loyalty attributes computed along the columns and the second table shows that of the loyalty determinants taken along the rows (rearranged in columns here). The bottom rows show the final averages of the three age groups that can be used as weights when assessing customer loyalty.

Observation of the above tables helps us examine the differences between different age groups on the perception of what generate customer loyalty and what determine loyalty. In some way, the loyalty determinants can be considered as the independent variables and the loyalty attributes as the dependent variables. All determinants can independently contribute to generate a specific type of loyalty attribute.

As far as the loyalty attributes are concerned (first table), brand benefit and brand convenience, with a weighting of 27% each, remain vital for generating customer loyalty. It means the brand's functional features that would deliver the expected benefits are as equally important as the brand (product) availability and convenience in generating loyalty. It does not mean that attributes such as brand value (monetary value and price stability) and brand image are not important. But both of these attributes with 23% weighting have been perceived as less important than benefit and convenience attributes. However, when examined the lower age group, image (34%) attributes and convenience (25%) attributes have been given more importance than the value and benefit attributes. This may also reveal that younger generation seems highly image conscious than the grown-ups and the price factor or value attributes seems less important in generating loyalty.

Similarly, in the second table of loyalty determinants, customer perception on the confidence factor stands out with 28% weighting as the leading determinant. Confidence refers to reliability of product or brand in delivering the benefits where successful performance reinforces customer confidence and therefore loyalty towards the brand. Company's commitment to deliver the best with highest level of satisfaction to customers is also seen as vital (25%

weighting) together with effective communication (24%) to inform the customer about promise, performance and commitment. Unlike in the case of loyalty attributes, age difference does not seem to have any significant impact on how the customers see the importance of loyalty determinants in general.

Appendix C: Case Study 2

The second case study was aimed at assessing the level of customer loyalty for the same brand (brand A) of instant coffee using the same market segment from the previous study in BILKENT. Therefore the survey instruments from the previous questionnaire needed modification in order to reflect the brands studied. The study was conducted using only a small sample of 100 respondents selected from the above preliminary study. In the previous study, after completing the survey, respondents were asked to indicate their preferred brands of instant coffee. In fact, brand A was the preferred brand of almost 58% of the respondents. When asked if they could be contacted for a follow up study, most of them agreed and contact information exchanged. Over a period of one month, the second study was conducted using a modified survey instruments for the C2-B segment as an example shown below:

Examples of Modified Survey Instruments

Characteristics	Instruments
Perceived reliability of brand 'A' in delivering benefits as promised.	I would continue to buy brand 'A' coffee because I can rely on it to deliver the benefits & attributes as promised (taste, quality, freshness and packing).
Successful brand (A) outcome and Satisfactory performance.	I would continue to buy brand 'A' coffee because its consumption leads to a successful outcome by providing the expected benefits satisfactorily

There were thirty-two survey instruments (in four sections related to the BVCI variables) all together. With a maximum score of 10 for each instrument, the maximum total score for each section is 80 or 320 for the whole survey. However, the chances are extremely less for any one section to get the total maximum score of 80. Similarly, the maximum total scores of the C variables are also 80. The findings of the BILKENT study for brand 'A' instant coffee is shown in the table below. All individual averages have been rounded to the nearest digit.

Table A:

Customer Loyalty Assessment for Brand 'A' Instant Coffee

Attributes and Determinants	Benefit	Value	Convenience	Image	Total Score
Conformity 1	6	5	6	7	
Conformity 2	6	5	6	7	48
Confidence 1	8	7	7	8	
Confidence 2	7	5	8	7	57
Commitment 1	6	5	7	5	
Commitment 2	7	5	7	5	47
Communication 1	7	6	6	8	
Communication 2	7	6	6	8	54
Total Score	54	44	53	55	206

Table B: Attribute-led (behavior) Loyalty Index

Scores/Index	Benefit	Value	Convenience	Image
Total Scores (1)	54(pot: 80)	44(pot: 80)	53 (pot: 80)	55(pot: 80)
Weighting (2)	0.27 (27%)	0.23 (23%)	0.27 (27%)	0.23 (23%)
LI (1x2) As a % (*)	14.58 -21.6 67.50	10.12 -18.4 55.00	14.31 -21.6 66.25	12.65 -18.4 68.75

(*) The percentage index is obtained by dividing loyalty index (example 14.58) by the maximum potential of 21.6 (80 x 27%).

The Attribute-led Loyalty Index: (composite) is therefore 14.58+10.12+14.31+12.65 = 51.66 (as a percentage out of 80 is 64.57%).

Table C: Determinant-led (attitude) Loyalty Index

Scores/ Index	Conformity	Confidence	Commitment	Communication
Total Scores	48 (pot: 80)	57(pot: 80)	47 (pot: 80)	54 (pot: 80)
Weighting	0.23 (23%)	0.28 (28%)	0.25 (25%)	0.24 (24%)
Loyalty Index As a % (*)	11.04 (18.4) 60.00	15.96 (22.4) 71.25	11.75 (20) 58.75	12.96 (19.2) 67.50

(*) The percentage index is obtained by dividing loyalty index (example 11.04) by the maximum potential of 18.4 (80 x 23%).

The Aggregate Determinant-led Loyalty Index: therefore is 11.04+15.96+11.75+12.96 = 51.71 (as a percentage out of 80 is 64.71%)

The Loyalty Indices

There are two loyalty indices: first and the obvious one is based on the attributes that are said to generate customer brand loyalty; the other consists of factors that determine the efforts the company makes to provide those attributes. The first loyalty index is therefore based on the BVCI attributes that leads to customer behavior in the market place. The second index is based on customers' attitude that is shaped up by their perception on company's efforts to deliver the attributes.

While both loyalty indices are important, marketers may see the attribute-led loyalty index as practical and useful. Whatever may be the case, it is useful to note the computation of individual indices for every BVCI attributes and C variables. In the case of the attribute-led loyalty indices (first table), the 'image' attribute leads with an index of 12.65 or 68.75 in percent (it is logical to refer to the percentage index). The benefit and convenience attributes come second and third with an index of 67.50 and 66.25 respectively. The value attribute with the lowest index of 55 stayed much lower than the image attribute.

This clearly shows that the customer loyalty for the brand 'A' instant coffee rested mainly with its brand image than anything else. However, the brand performance and availability also contributed to generating customer loyalty for the brand. In fact, the brand studied here was a well-known brand and the company, a multinational corporation, spends millions of dollars in advertising and building a prestigious brand image all over the world. The market segment studied being an affluent image-conscious group of people, it is not surprising that the loyalty towards the product would depend more on its brand image and performance than anything else. The overall aggregate attribute-led customer loyalty index is the sum of BVCI indices, which stood at 51.66 or 64.57 in percentage.

As far as the loyalty determinants of C variables are concerned (the second table), confidence (71.25) and communication (67.50) factors are perceived to be important by the customer in generating attitudinal loyalty. However, conformity (60.00) and commitment (58.75) factors are not perceived as less important either. This clearly shows that customers placed more emphasis on company's effort to generate confidence by being reliable in delivering the attributes such as brand image and product benefits as promised. The overall aggregate attitudinal loyalty index is 51.74 or 61.74 as a percentage.

Index Page

1627542R0

Printed in Great Britain
by Amazon.co.uk, Ltd.,
Marston Gate.